'Interested in content and drama form, *Imagining the Real* takes a long hard look at drama teaching in the 20th and 21st centuries and questions whether we are moving backwards instead of forwards. Concerned about the widespread adoption of a potentially reductive conventions approach, Davis takes the reader on a thrilling socio-political, historical and ideological critique of the big issues pervading drama in education since its inception. Inspired by Edward Bond's concern for understanding the world and ourselves in it, Davis is interested in developing a relevant form of post-Brechtian (non-distanced) drama for young people, and this book provides readers with a unique insight into the aims, purposes and processes of drama teaching from one of its greatest proponents. Skilfully interweaving his highly engaging narrative with practical examples and a wealth of references from philosophy, cultural theory, political science, economics, education and the arts, the reader will emerge with a well-balanced critique of contemporary drama theory and practice, and a framework for Davis's own tried and tested approach developed over a lifetime of commitment to the art of drama teaching with young people. Featuring some of the best explanations I have ever read on role play, frame distancing, sequencing, modes of involvement, protection into role, and Bond's new theory of making drama, this is an absolute must-read for all involved in classroom drama teaching and in research in the field. It sows the seeds for a much-needed re-engagement and re-envisioning of drama in education in the 21st century.'

**Professor Carmel O'Sullivan, Head of the School of
Education, Trinity College Dublin, Ireland**

'Written by one of the most important figures in drama in education, Davis will provoke necessary discussion about dramatic conventions and form, ideology and globalization, as well as the political imperatives that should power teaching. A required reference for all interested in the field's history and future directions, and what it means to be an engaged educator for the 21st century.'

**Professor Philip Taylor, Steinhardt School of Culture, Education,
and Human Development, New York University, USA**

'This book goes far beyond the other books available, which only provide drama activities with teacher-dominated exercises. It is basically a theory-based book and can be used as a great textbook for undergraduate and graduate level education. David draws readers' attention to how to build direct engagement in drama events, which may lead to meaningful learning. I believe that it will be a valuable resource for Turkish drama teachers and will fill an important gap in the drama in education area.'

Professor Dr Ulku Koymen, European University of Lefke, Cyprus

'*Imagining the Real* is an inspiring book lighting up a new horizon for drama in education not just in Britain but internationally.

This book comes out of a very deep experience of working with students, teachers and artists and it allows us as practitioners in the field of drama in education to re-examine, not just our practices, but the theories behind those practices.

The importance of this book is that it provides us with the opportunity to explore anew the nature of humanity, justice and freedom through a new understanding of the role of the arts in the present epoch. In particular it opens a new dialogue and asks new questions to create a continuous dialogue between education and drama as an art form.'

Wasim Kurdi, Director of the Centre for Educational Research and Development, Al Qattan Foundation, Ramallah, Palestine

'It has been almost two decades since drama in education was first introduced to Hong Kong and mainland China through the teaching of Professor Davis. Like an adolescent growing up into a mature person, drama in education practitioners here (including myself) are in a transitional stage, hungering for new thoughts and rebellious stimulation to imagine a new drama in education vision for our generation. This publication is such a timely, refreshing and inspiring gift to meet our growing needs, and will definitely become one of the most influential books on the development of drama education in Chinese communities.'

Estella Wong, Senior Lecturer (Academic Studies in Drama) and MFA Coordinator (Drama), Hong Kong Academy for Performing Arts, China

'Nowadays, educational drama is flourishing in Korea. For educational drama to develop in its true sense, critical and reflective perspectives are needed. This book will play that role. Full of stimulating questions and reflections, it is a timely work much needed for the current Korean educational drama scene.'

Dr Ju-Yoon Kim, Seoul National University of Education, South Korea

'The distinction between 'I want to be grown up' and 'I want to grow up' lies at the heart of this text. In understanding that difference, we perceive the urgency of Davis's passionate, considered contribution towards a new theorizing of drama as education.'

Professor Juliana Saxton, University of Victoria, Canada

'There is an obvious need internationally for a recontextualization of drama, defining its aims and tools based on the problems and challenges we face in the 21st century. David Davis does this with passion in his book, connecting theory and practice, art and pedagogy in drama in education. The thorough critique of his own work, besides that of others in the field, shows his dedication to the development of our field. The questions raised by the book need to be addressed by drama teachers and theatre in education practitioners, not just in the UK and Hungary, but around the world.'

Adam Bethlenfalvy, Director, InSite Drama, Budapest, Hungary

'David Davis's book is a timely one that serves several important functions. For one, it acts as a sage guide, taking the reader carefully through a personal history of drama teaching, tracing the pioneering work of Dorothy Heathcote and Gavin Bolton in a trajectory that leads us to a fascinating practical exploration and assessment of Edward Bond's innovatory drama for young people. Here, Davis's analysis is always clear-sighted and always concerned to demonstrate how theory can be applied practically within the classroom. The book is also an unapologetic, passionate and uncompromising call to arms in its advocacy for the central place that the teaching of drama should occupy within the National Curriculum. This comes at a time when its future has never been so uncertain. Subsequently, this book will inform, rally and inspire.'

Dr Graham Saunders, Department of Film, Theatre & Television, University of Reading, UK

'In the past decades drama in education has seemed to be at a standstill. Davis's book is rejuvenating by offering an inspirational new beginning. It breaks new ground in the area and at the same time it is an indispensable must-read for beginners. In the Greek context, where process drama is still developing and in its preliminary stages, this book can push forward Greek teachers' theory and practice. The book illustrates, in the best possible way, complex concepts that traverse drama, politics, philosophy, and pedagogy in a reader-friendly way.'

Dr Kostas Amoiropoulos, Director, Diadromes Drama Studio, Athens, Greece

To my grandsons Theo and Leon and my step-grandchildren Ettie and Jake

Imagining the Real

IOEPress Trentham Books

Imagining the Real

Towards a new theory of drama in education

David Davis

Foreword by Gavin Bolton
Afterword by Mike Fleming

A Trentham Book
Institute of Education Press

First published in 2014 by the Institute of Education Press, University of London, 20 Bedford Way, London WC1H 0AL

ioepress.co.uk

British Library Cataloguing in Publication Data:
A catalogue record for this publication is available from the British Library

ISBNs
978-1-85856-513-2 (paperback)
978-1-85856-641-2 (PDF eBook)
978-1-85856-642-9 (ePub eBook)
978-1-85856-643-6 (Kindle eBook)

Typeset by Quadrant Infotech (India) Pvt Ltd
Printed and bound by CPI Group (UK) Ltd, Croydon, CR0 4YY

Cover image by Ceri Townsend, © Big Brum Theatre in Education Company. Reproduced by permission.

Contents

List of figures

Acknowledgements

I am very conscious that a new generation of drama teachers and theatre in education workers is researching the same area, investigating how Edward Bond's drama theory and practice works and how can it be used in drama in education. All are equally committed to driving this process forward; writers Chris Cooper, Kostas Amoiropoulos, Adam Bethlenfalvy, John Doona and Kate Katafiasz among others are all in different ways working in the same area. I feel confident that they will be able to develop this work much further than I can.

I am deeply indebted to Chris Cooper, who has read drafts of the book as it has been written and given valuable feedback, and, of course, for his help with the last section of the book, which we worked on together.

I owe a lifetime of indebtedness to Gavin Bolton, who was my first real teacher and remained an inspiration for the whole of my teaching life. We have shared over 45 years of teaching and learning together – he doing the teaching and I doing the learning – plus many adventures in New York and various other locations while we were teaching together. And many thanks to him for writing the Foreword. My very deep thanks also to Edward Bond, my second great teacher. He is a constant source of creative striving, and the regular contact over many years has been a source of illumination to me. He read a draft of the book and fed back many useful comments. This book is really a homage to these two individuals who, in their own, different ways, are dedicated to creating a human future.

My especial thanks go to all those at the Al Qattan Foundation Centre for Educational Research and Development in Ramallah, Palestine. The Director, Wasim Kurdi, has constantly made the resources of the Centre available to me and made it possible for me to continue working in drama with so many people in Palestine and in the Al Qattan Summer School in Jordan. My especial thanks go to the research team in Palestine that I have worked with for the last two years: Mutasem, Vivian, Raida, Yousef and Amira. And of course to my special friend, Kifah, who has been translator, friend and support over many years.

Thanks also to my many friends in the Turkish Association and especially its President, Professor Ömer Adıgüzel, and my wonderful translator and friend, Dr Selen Korad Birkiye. Over recent years I have frequently been invited to run workshops and give keynotes and I have come to view the

Contemporary Drama Association as the most impressive drama education organization that I know of internationally.

My thanks to John Airs who patiently wrote up his notes on my teaching at the Jordan Summer School; to Mike Fleming, for being there whenever I needed him; to Carmel O'Sullivan, for always supporting my work through thick and thin; to Oylum Akkus Ispir and Alec Kimble, for checking the maths; to Bill Roper, for many long discussions on imagination and related topics, which must have driven him to distraction; to Richard Hatcher, for being the ideal colleague to have, constantly prompting new thinking; to my long-standing colleagues and friends in China, Li Yingning, Estella Wong and Phoebe Chan; and to Ceri Townsend for her inspirational cover design.

My special thanks to Gillian Klein, who has been a constant source of support, and a beacon of hope in the publishing field.

I also have to thank my many students, stretching down the years, who have taught me so much.

Most important of all are my thanks and love to my wife Elaine who is a total constant in my life. And to my lovely daughter, also Elaine, who has cheered her dad on in the writing of this book.

I will have missed out many more. I hope they will forgive me.

Foreword

It is over forty years since I welcomed David into the University of Durham's postgraduate course for experienced teachers, promoting the development of drama education in schools. From those early days our careers seem to have coincided as we became temporary colleagues in various short courses in the UK and Canada and I became a visiting lecturer and examiner on his own course in Birmingham. I have always enjoyed his company and appreciated his continuing support for my work, culminating with his recent publication of my *Essential Writings* (2010). So much of his writing, as he moved from lecturer to professor and then (astonishingly!) to semi-*retired* professor, has given us a glimpse of his perspective on the development, or lack of it, of drama in education. Only now are we being shown the full picture of his own vision of the field.

When he asked me to contribute to this publication, I was a bit taken aback as I thought I had made it clear to everyone some years ago that my professional career is over. Indeed I have firmly (and, often, with some regret) turned down similar invitations in recent years. But here was David, sitting in our lounge … so what could I do?

Some weeks later, when he sent me two-thirds of the script, I sat at my desk with a strong sense of 'duty', thinking 'Well, I'd better get started …' I did not realize that I would find myself not wanting to put it down! I have found it totally absorbing. Here was a new world of thinking, reaching beyond anything I had read before. I feel like a student again, with David as my teacher.

The reader can sense, from its early pages, that this book, with its firmly political introduction, is going to be groundbreaking, seeking a different perspective on how drama can lead to the opening up of 'a new form of consciousness'. In a profound way David is reaching beyond an exploration of Drama, important as that is: he is appealing to all teachers to recognize the much-needed change in values if society is to escape its current cultural trap – and Drama Education is one of the routes that can take the next generation into a more caring and more responsible direction.

David is offering an entirely new theory of classroom drama and theatre-in-education, a theory that invites a different focus for teachers. The pathway he is inviting us to examine is linked closely with the work of the UK contemporary playwright Edward Bond, whose approach to theatre fundamentally challenges the traditions we associate with Stanislavski and

Brecht. David suggests there is some connection between Bond's art and the kind of 'living through' drama that Dorothy Heathcote introduced to us some fifty years ago, for it is 'being *in* the event' that provides that common ground. Because I pursued and tried to refine this particular approach for most of my career, David has used my work as a means of underpinning his application of Bond's concept of drama to drama in schools.

This is a remarkable publication, breaking completely new ground and, 'fellow teachers', I think we have a lot to learn.

Gavin Bolton

The future of our species depends on one and only one thing: that the Imagination of the adult should be as free as the imagination of the child. Then the adult will Imagine the real – that is, create value in the world of facts. In doing this the adult will take responsibility for the world: he or she will become part of the map of the world. When adults Imagine the real they become human: otherwise they are not human – the Imagination is owned by the state and produced as Ideology, the falsehoods behind which are the fairy tales of murderers.

(Bond, 2000: 101)

What is here?
Gold? Yellow, glittering, precious gold? ...
Thus much of this will make black white, foul fair,
Wrong right, base noble, old young, coward valiant. ...

This yellow slave
Will knit and break religions, bless th'accursed,
Make the hoar leprosy adored, place thieves
And give them title, knee and approbation
With senators on the bench ...

(Shakespeare, *Timon of Athens*, IV, iii)

Drama is events occurring on a site. The site is the scene of some particular human and social problem. The problem is specific but ultimately the site is the whole of society and human reality. It stretches from the kitchen table to the edge of the universe.

(Bond, 2013a: 35)

Introduction

> A dog starved at his master's gate,
> Predicts the ruin of the state.
>
> (William Blake)

Some years ago I expressed my concern that drama in education[1] had reached a problematic point in its development and was 'in a siding' (Davis, 2005: 166). It seemed to be in stasis after the years of progress under Dorothy Heathcote and Gavin Bolton. Now it seems to be regressing. I argue in that publication that we need to return to the early Heathcote and the late Bolton and develop form with the influence of Edward Bond's work in theatre. The crucial element I am seeking to develop, following Bolton, is the *direct* engagement in role of the individual in the drama event, not involvement from a distanced perspective. This direct engagement needs to be embedded in a form of drama that, following Bond, will confront the individual with the actual social forces that are operating in that particular situation: to see through the ideological distortions that disrupt our vision. The aim is to provoke the opportunity to find one's relationship to those social forces, thus providing an opening for us each to create our own humanness – the central aim of Bond's theatre. This book examines and attempts to advance this thesis.

As the crisis in culture has developed it has put ever more pressure on teachers to produce measurable results. As with the rest of society, education is driven by market forces and consequently our awareness of human values and consciousness is threatened. Edward Bond calls this the third crisis:

> We are in the third of the crises in which a new form of consciousness must be created so that society can function and still be human. The earlier crises were the Greek and Jacobean. Both created a new drama – Greek tragedy and democracy, Jacobean tragedy and the first modern self. The third crisis has prised the existing human consciousness away from society's technology and administration. We can't humanly *apprehend* what we are doing on our site, we are sleep walkers walking towards death and the world begins to creak like a coffin.
>
> (Bond, 2013a: 13)

A few writers on drama teaching have drawn attention to globalization but have been unable to do more than recommend that young people be better prepared to live in a globalized world. Some have tried to develop forms of theatre that use space differently, influenced by performance theory. I return to both of these later. However, as far as I have been able to ascertain, none of the recent writers on drama in education has been able to deal with the fundamental problem of ideology and the urgent need to forge a new consciousness. As Bond argues:

> All cultures interpret reality through the extravagant use of imagination and this means that reality is imagined and so imaginary. That's a definition of madness but also of societies.
>
> (Bond, 2013a: 38)

We are culturally insane. We are complicit in driving ourselves and the planet to destruction. We have glimpses of what is happening and momentarily look to see if there is a brake but then let those in power crack the whip and hurtle us more rapidly into the crisis. Unless we get greater clarity about our situation and develop new forms of drama we only aid the process of self-destruction.

In recent publications on drama teaching I have found scant reference to these changing times and the challenges posed. Where they are raised it is, as I mention above, in the context of globalization. One such example is to be found in Anderson (2012): 'The book argues that schooling, schools and students are changing and teachers must respond to this change by transforming their approach to drama education' (Anderson, 2012: 1). This sounds interesting. However, the social change is presented as the digital revolution. The answer is for the N-Gen (Generation Next) as digital natives to work with the digital immigrants (the teachers). Anderson argues that the 'N-Gen students are literally wired differently from previous generations' (20). This echoes Greenfield's concerns (see for example, Greenfield, 2009) and makes them sound like a breed apart. Greenfield offers no significant research to back her claims and neither does Anderson. I would see every human being as wired differently. Every generation has had new challenges from technological change. Flying a supersonic jet fighter will need a differently configured brain to the brain of the ploughman. The new generation may have more ability in handling digital technology than previous generations but this is from practice and does not mean they are qualitatively different as humans, that they have lost their human essence. As they build up their network on Facebook it seems more that they have found a new way to be part of a gang, to belong, which has its positive dimensions, and to gain an identity (which invites a multitude of questions). It seems to me that professionals do the same on LinkedIn. The more contacts you have, the more you exist: an attempt to overcome our social alienation which, in fact, only increases it. iPhone therefore I am. Adults as well as young people are never away from their smartphones: the more people who phone us the more we exist. The 'high' and the 'mighty', as well as the person in the street, all Twitter away.

I do not see that the greater familiarity young people have with new technology makes them a breed apart. With the click of a mouse I too have access to millions of pages of information. What does seem to be happening is a change in cultural identity: we are being driven apart and losing our sense of community, becoming atomized in the process. The mind shift that is taking place is one where we are becoming the willing servants of neo-liberal values. This seems to me to be the main danger from the new technology. However, it also presents us with great possibilities but it depends on how this technology is used and in whose interests. Anderson quotes John O'Toole:

> As we hurtle into the millennium, Hong Kong, Japan, Singapore and Australia too, the worlds of corporation and government are beginning to realize that preparedness for change is the biggest challenge facing us and the next generations; to embrace creativity and teamwork, designers, artists, musicians and performing arts consultants are in demand and short supply. There's a desperate urge to find people who can hypothesise ... empathise, think laterally, make fictional models of possible realities and communicate them to others – all the core business of drama.
>
> (O'Toole, 2002 cited in Anderson, 2012: 101)

This seems to me to miss the point. I cannot see the purpose of drama as helping young people become the servants of this globalized economy. Drama is not in the business of moulding young minds to embrace the values and mindset that drives massive corporations to plunder the world's resources in pursuit of profit.

So what sort of education do we need to avoid sleepwalking towards death, and how does drama fit into that education? This book is an attempt to wrestle with these concerns.

Part One offers some evidence for the seriousness of our situation and the inadequacy of current forms of theatre, drama in education and applied theatre. I adopt Bond's thesis that we have not yet developed a post-Brechtian drama that can act as a force in the current crisis of humanity. Rather, we are still repeating Stanislaviskian, Brechtian and Performance Theatre forms. In particular, I argue that drama in education remains, for the most part, trapped in a reflective mode, echoing a form of Brechtian distancing exemplified by the conventions approach developed mainly by Jonothan Neelands.

In Part Two I set out some aspects of the approach to drama in education that I have developed over the years and which has been influenced principally by Gavin Bolton and Dorothy Heathcote. I do not have the space to detail every area that concerns a drama teacher: that would need a whole book to itself. I have confined myself to key areas important to enabling 'living through' drama experiences. This makes the drama focus of the book centre around what Bolton terms 'making' drama (Bolton, 2010c: 38–40)[2] and which he describes as 'a hugely important educational and dramatic tool' (43). My predominant interest has been in drama in education as an art form rather than theatre for performance or drama for curriculum teaching and learning, although these have also been important to me. My aim in detailing my own approach to 'making' drama is so that I can begin to analyse it.

Part Three is an attempt to start developing a new theory of drama in education by reviewing the drama components that are used to construct the major process drama example in Part Two; this analysis is influenced by the new form of theatre developed by Edward Bond. I am aided here by Chris Cooper, who has worked closely with Bond over some 18 years and knows his work better than anyone else in the UK.

In my first 25 years of drama teaching, my attempts at finding form were influenced chiefly by Gavin Bolton and Dorothy Heathcote and, in the latter 20 years, Edward Bond increasingly became my major influence. This book is, therefore, primarily about form in school drama. It is not a guide to teaching drama in relation to any national curriculum but focuses on drama as an art form and aims to be useful to teachers, not just in the UK but teachers anywhere who are using drama to help young people find themselves in the world and the world in them. Its aims are to place the problem and then attempt to do no more than make a start in a new direction.

Both Part One and Part Three have theoretical introductions, in which I attempt to share the thinking underpinning what follows. Some of the areas may seem at first to be rather distant from my main concern, which is form in classroom drama. I ask the reader to bear with me. I hope I can convince you that the areas I deal with *are* relevant.

I suspect that the trend in education in recent years has been to squeeze out time for wide reading and discovery of exciting ideas in favour of time spent cramming facts and information for examinations. I was lucky enough to have been at school in the 1950s when the progressive period of education was just beginning. I can remember at the age of 12 being enthralled by a teacher discussing the red shift and realizing for the first time that the universe was expanding at a phenomenal rate. This was not in a science lesson but a general knowledge lesson. I can remember the excitement of discussing 'Did God make man or did man make God?'[3] in an after-school discussion club run jointly by two teachers, a Quaker and an atheist, both of whom encouraged open thinking and questioning. Numerous other examples come to mind but one in particular stands out. While studying A-level English our forward-looking teacher brought in a book with a brown paper wrapper to hide the original cover. He spent an hour reading us a chapter and we were enthralled by the description of nature it depicted and the richness of the language. After we had discussed it at length he revealed it was D.H. Lawrence's *Lady Chatterley's Lover*, a book banned at the time by the strict censorship laws in the UK, and which he had smuggled into the country from Sweden. The class discussed the pros and cons of censorship. Intrigued by the chapter, I asked if I could borrow the book. After only a moment's hesitation he agreed, on condition I kept it secret. I read it and before the year was out had read every Lawrence novel I could find. I was 18 at the time and old enough to die for my country but forbidden from reading a serious work of literature. I cannot imagine anything as progressive as passing me that book happening today and it is that change in mindset that is a key concern of this book. It was the Quaker teacher who passed it to me.

As a young teacher I was guided by books such as *Teaching as a Subversive Activity* (Postman and Weingartner, 1971). It is only subversive of the aftermath of the rigid education system of the 1930s that was rapidly being thrown out in the post-war period (it was written in 1967). It is in fact a manual for progressive teaching methods:

> We are simple, professional educators, which means that we are simple, romantic men who risk contributing to the mental health problem by maintaining a belief in the improvability of the human condition through education.
>
> (Postman and Weingartner, 1971: 12)

> If it is irrelevant ... if it shields children from reality ... if it educates for obsolescence ... if it does not develop intelligence ... if it is

> based on fear ... if it avoids promotion of significant learning ...
> if it punishes creativity and independence ... it *must* be changed.
>
> (Postman and Weingartner, 1971: 13, emphasis in original)

I had the good fortune at one stage in my school-teaching days to be Head of Drama and part of an English department that was led by John O'Toole, and included in it Mike Fleming, Geoff Gillham, John Spinks, John Grundy and many other vibrant young teachers. (John O'Toole and Mike Fleming became professors and leading figures in the drama education world, Geoff Gillham became the leading figure in Theatre in Education and a well-known playwright, John Spinks is now a well-known artist with a studio under the Brooklyn Bridge and John Grundy became an architecture writer and television presenter.) It was a lively department! We had time in weekly meetings to discuss books and ideas. For example, when Ivan Illich's book *Deschooling Society* came out, we discussed it. When the *Bullock Report (A Language for Life)* came out, we had a whole-school staff meeting to discuss it. When I went into higher education and the *Black Papers* were published, the Faculty of Education had a whole-staff seminar to defend progressive education from the attacks in those papers – the first attacks on progressive education, which eventually led to the destruction of all the positives of that movement.

I pay homage to these times not out of nostalgia (although that is tempting) but to make a point. I cannot imagine schools today having the time or agenda to allow the sort of excitement of learning I describe above. The culture of our times has changed dramatically. It is this crisis of culture that I want to address in the following pages. The apparent digressions in the introductions that follow are germane to my argument and attempt to recover some of that discussion that there no longer seems time for in our schools today: the key concerns of our epoch.

Notes

[1] I always chose to refer to drama in education without capitals. I simply mean all drama in an educational context. There is not a single body of work that could be given the proper noun Drama in Education.

[2] I am using this latest edition of Bolton's writing as much of his writing is now out of print.

[3] Women were excluded in those days, so they will be relieved to hear that if man made the world women bear no responsibility for the mess it is in.

Part One

1

Chapter 1
The context

I'm an unashamed traditionalist when it comes to the curriculum. Most parents would rather their children had a traditional education, with children sitting in rows, learning the kings and queens of England, the great works of literature, proper mental arithmetic, algebra by the age of eleven, modern foreign languages. That's the best training of the mind and that's how children will be able to compete.

(The Times, 6 March 2010)

So said the current Secretary of State for Education in the UK, Michael Gove, the person responsible for education in this country. It is the statement of someone who wants to return education to the condition satirized by Charles Dickens in *Hard Times* in 1854; someone who promotes the passive role of the pupil learning facts; who seeks to bypass all the gains in teaching and learning theory in the last one hundred years or so, from Dewey (1897) 'I believe the active side precedes the passive …' (Hickmann and Alexander, 1998: 233) to Bruner (1996) 'The teacher … is a guide to understanding, someone who helps you *discover on your own*' (xii, my emphasis). Gove's educational 'vision' wants children sitting in neat rows listening to talk and chalk. It is nationalistic and narrow, sees education as training, and harks back to a discredited form of faculty psychology with a belief that learning facts in a range of disciplines somehow trains the mind across different areas of learning: the reason that used to be put forward for learning Latin in the school curriculum. While attending a recent conference, a well-known professor of education said to me in passing 'Gove is an educational ignoramus'. Far be it from me to repeat such slanderous comment – but it made me think.

Gove explains that one of the 'biggest influences on [his] thinking about education reform has been the American cognitive scientist Daniel T. Willingham' and 'his quite brilliant book *Why Don't Students Like School?*' (Gove, 2012).

In his book, Willingham (2009) claims that the brain and mind are synonymous, that we are not naturally good thinkers as 'the mind is not designed for thinking' but 'designed for the avoidance of thought'

(Willingham, 2009: 4) and totally misses out the cultural development of higher mental processes. He claims that Einstein is wrong to assert that imagination is more important than knowledge. For him, 'Knowledge is more important' (47). He argues that the more facts you accumulate the more you know (44–5) and finishes the book with the following statement, 'Education is the passing on of the accumulated wisdom of generations to children, and we passionately believe in its importance because we know that it holds the promise of a better life for each child, and for us all, collectively' (213). In other words, 'We are wise. We have the knowledge. We will pass it on.' This would satisfy any totalitarian regime! Bruner destroys this sort of approach in his book *The Culture of Education* (1996) where he argues against a purely cognitive approach and transmission teaching and argues instead for interactive sharing, active learning and questioning and the teacher as guide to the pupils' self-construction.

Gove is fond of referring to Finland as a good educational model to follow. In the Foreword to his 2010 White Paper he draws attention to the excellence of aspects of education in Finland that have been an inspiration to him. And Finland deserves that tribute. In a global league table produced by the Economist Intelligence Unit for Pearson they found Finland to have the best education system in the world. The rankings combined international test results between 2006 and 2010.

However, in typical Gove fashion, he is very selective with the facts and details. Usefully, Pasi Sahlberg, who works at the Finnish Ministry of Education, has put the record straight in *Finnish Lessons* (2011), his fascinating study of the development of their education system:

> Finland is an example of a nation that lacks school inspection, standardized curriculum, high-stakes student assessment, test-based accountability, and a race to the top mentality with regard to educational change. ... [Finland *opposes*] tightening controls over schools, stronger accountability for student performance, firing bad teachers, and doing down troubled schools.
>
> (Sahlberg, 2011: 4–5, my emphasis)

To repeat, just for the pleasure of it, Finland has no Ofsted (the UK's Office for Standards in Education, Children's Services and Skills) visiting schools, observing teachers, and judging teaching and management, grading them and the schools, with powers to place the school in special measures as a failing school. Finland has no standardized tests; no league tables to pit school against school and teacher against teacher; no payment by results;

instead, teachers are highly respected and supported. And, again, just for the pleasure of it:

> All of the factors behind Finnish success seem to be the opposite of what is taking place in the US and much of the rest of the world, where competition, test-based accountability, standardization, and privatization seem to dominate.
>
> (Sahlberg, 2011: 11)

What is more, as the Economist Intelligence Unit (2012) reports, teachers in Finland are afforded the same status as doctors and lawyers. Children are not tested at all for the first six years of their education. There is only one mandatory standardized test in Finland, taken at age 16. All children are taught in mixed-ability classrooms. Finland spends around 30 per cent less per student than the United States. By the time they leave school 'over half of all students have received some sort of special education, personalized help, or individual guidance' (Sahlberg, 2011: 11). That is to say, individual educational needs, from support in mathematics lessons to support in language development, are regarded as a norm and are addressed and supported. Science classes are capped at 16 students so that they may perform practical experiments in every class. Teachers spend four hours a day in the classroom, and take two hours a week for professional development. The school system is 100 per cent state funded. All teachers in Finland must have a master's degree, and study for it is fully subsidized. The national curriculum is only broad guidelines. Teachers are selected from the top 10 per cent of graduates. There is no merit pay for teachers. Finnish children do not start school until they are 7. They rarely take examinations or do homework until they are well into their teens. (I did enjoy writing that!)

One wonders whether Gove actually read anything about Finnish education apart from the fact that they had the best test results internationally.

First and foremost Gove sees education as serving the globalized economy. His agenda is political, not educational, and this sets a challenge to anyone writing about education today. It would be irresponsible not to write a political book on the subject, just as it would be irresponsible not to seek to understand how the political enwraps all we do, including drama teaching. This book about drama in education is, therefore, political. I am in good company here: 'However much it may be claimed to the contrary, education is always political ...' (Bruner, 1996: 25).

In outlining the present political situation as the impetus and need for this book, I am conscious that the situation will be different tomorrow and there is a danger in being too precise about the state we are in. By the time the book is published the situation is likely to be markedly different and almost certainly worse. In the Introduction I quoted Edward Bond calling it the 'third crisis'. It is an economic, environmental, political and above all a cultural crisis. As Bond states in the earlier quotation 'a new form of consciousness must be created so that society can function and still be human' (Bond, 2013a: 13). To aid the struggle for this new form of consciousness we need a new drama and a new drama in education.

It may be useful to begin with a look at the economic dimension – hardly the usual way to start a book on drama teaching. I am not an economist so write only from an everyday understanding and offer a perspective for consideration. I am starting in this way just as some drama educators start from the fact that the educational environment is a globalized one.

Globalization and the neo-liberal agenda

> The ... received wisdom is that the second half of the twentieth century, the very heart and soul of our 2,500 year old civilization is, apparently, economic, and from that heart flowed, and continues to flow, everything else. We must therefore fling down and fling up the structures of our society as the marketplace orders. If we don't, the marketplace will do it anyway.
>
> (Saul, 1997: 3)

It is broadly accepted that we live in a period of globalization.

> Globalisation describes a process by which national and regional economies, societies, and cultures have become integrated through the global network of trade, communication, immigration and transportation.

> In the more recent past, globalisation was often primarily focused on the economic side of the world, such as trade, foreign direct investment and international capital flows, more recently the term has been expanded to include a broader range of areas and activities such as culture, media, technology, socio-cultural, political, and even biological factors, e.g. climate change.
>
> (Financial Times Lexicon)

It is the scope and range of globalization portrayed in the last sentence that especially interests me: globalization influences every corner of our lives; it is taking us over. The only key area missing from the above is the personal, although that is implied by 'socio-cultural'. I am aware that the migration referred to above is certainly personal – some 215 million migrants are travelling the world at this moment – economic migrants in the main but also refugees and asylum seekers (Migration Policy Institute Data Hub), just part of the displacement and disruption of people in the service of capital. For sure, globalization is influencing education policy and every teacher in every school. In Europe this is spelled out very clearly. The European Commissioner for Education's website claims:

> Improvements in education, research and innovation are needed:
>
> • to help Europe compete globally
> • to equip the young for today's job market
> • to address the consequence of the economic crisis.
>
> (Cited in Hirtt, 2011: 7)

This is elaborated in a European document published in 2009 with the title *Key Competences for a Changing World*:

> • Education and training should become more open and relevant to the needs of the labour market.
> • Particular attention should be given to establishing partnerships between the worlds of education and training and that of work.
> • The economic downturn puts these long-term challenges even more into the spotlight.
> • More than ever Europe's success in global competition is dependent on its skills and innovation capacities.
> • The role of education and training underpinning the knowledge triangle needs to be reinforced. Innovation and growth will be weak without a broad foundation of knowledge, skills and competences.
>
> (cited in Hirtt, 2011: 8, punctuation as in original)

The European and US economies are in crisis. We all know this, especially in countries like Ireland, Greece, Spain, Portugal, Cyprus, and now in the UK. But how did we get here? It is, perhaps, worth going back to an earlier period to trace some of the major developments in the Western economies.

There was a boom in the USA after the First World War, referred to as 'the Roaring Twenties'. It lasted about eight years and then crashed in 1929. The banks had got out of control and were lending money to people to buy stocks at only a small percentage of their real cost. This was fine while confidence lasted, but when it collapsed, people tried to withdraw their money and the banks did not have the means to cover the amount of the withdrawals. In other words, the banks had dreamed up schemes to enable people to buy shares without needing to find the full amount to pay for them – a scheme doomed to failure. (Sound familiar?) In 1933 the banks were regulated under the Glass-Steagall Act, which separated the casino investment side of the banks from their savings side. It could be argued that the slump of the 1930s, which initiated a worldwide depression and was caused in large part by the greed of the bankers, fed directly into the social crises that gave rise to fascism in Germany, Italy, Japan, and Spain and, ultimately, to the Second World War. This is a simplification but I would maintain there is a strong kernel of truth here.

After the horrors of the Second World War, the public mood in the UK was set for social reform. The Labour Party was voted into power in 1945 and sang 'The Red Flag' at the opening of Parliament. (How times change!) Industries were nationalized. Rampant capitalism seemed to be in retreat. The Welfare State was established with the National Health Service as the flagship achievement. Progressive ideas were afoot in education, leading to the policy of comprehensive education: aiming for an equal education opportunity for all. Peter Slade was arguing for Child Drama. Capitalism was forced, temporarily, to adopt an element of social justice into its agenda. This was an early attempt at what became known later as 'The Third Way' – an attempt to put a human face to capitalism; an oxymoronic phrase if ever there was one.

However, the industries nationalized were failing through lack of investment and needed modernizing (at the taxpayers' expense) in order to service the rest of the economy. Later the Conservative Party had the gains in social welfare in their sights and the nationalized industries, now modernized, were ripe for privatization. Enter the free market. In the 1980s, under Margaret Thatcher in the UK and Ronald Reagan in the US, the process began of promoting what became neo-liberal economics. Their economic guru was Milton Friedman, the arch-proponent of free-market economies who argued for privatization and minimum state interference. This would lead to prosperity for all. Naomi Klein (2007) destroys this myth in her excellently researched book *The Shock Doctrine*.

Friedmanite policies led to the disempowering of the unions and privatization of many corporations over successive Conservative governments: parts of British Aerospace and Cable & Wireless in the first place, followed by Jaguar, British Telecom, the remainder of Cable & Wireless and British Aerospace, Britoil and British Gas, and subsequently British Steel, British

Petroleum, Rolls Royce, British Airways, water and electricity, and British Coal, as well as electricity generating companies Powergen and National Power, and British Rail. Billions of pounds went back into the Treasury but nowhere near the same amount of public money that had gone into buying them in the first place and then modernizing them. Labour continued with the privatizing policies under the name of the Private Finance Initiative, whereby hospitals and schools were built by private capital that had to be paid back over many years, making them much more expensive than if they had been built with public money (see Seymour, 2012).

However, the main beneficiary of these Friedmanite policies was the finance community. In 1986 the Conservative government under Margaret Thatcher introduced a package of new rules relaxing the regulation on the London Stock Exchange (known as the Big Bang). The City of London, the square mile housing most of the city's financial institutions, soon became the most profitable and most expensive place on the planet. Financial institutions flocked to the City to benefit from the deregulation. This deregulation fed a credit consumer boom. We became what we bought, all fuelled by credit.

Not to be outdone, in 1997 Gordon Brown, the Chancellor of the Exchequer, and his assistant Ed Balls, decided to deregulate the banks. Up to this point, the banks had been governed by strong regulatory structures also put in place since the Great Depression of 1929. No longer! Not to be left out of the race for cash, the Clinton administration, with Republican support, repealed the Glass-Steagall Act, in place since 1933. It was a free for all!

Once the banks were deregulated the finance industry spiralled out of control. 'In 2000, the total GDP [Gross Domestic Product] of earth – the sum total of all the economic activity – was $36 trillion. By the end of 2006, it was $70 trillion' (Lanchester, 2010: xii). This was, in part, fuelled by the enormous growth in the Chinese and Indian economic booms but also by the banks creating more and more credit. In his book, Lanchester explains in simple terms that even I could understand, how the banks dreamed up phony schemes to generate fictitious capital to provide credit. Bankers had weekends away to invent ever more obscure ways of creating these schemes. To take just one of Lanchester's examples – ordinary mortgages were already insured against loss, however, in the US to be able to insure the massive market in sub-prime mortgages (lending to people who normally would not qualify for a mortgage) a new form of insurance was needed, a new form of Collatoralized Debt Obligation, and lo and behold, a very clever person working at J.P. Morgan applied a Gaussian copula function to allow high-risk loans to appear to be covered by insurance. The formula looks like this (Lanchester, 2010: 97):

$$C_p(u,v = \varnothing_p) \, (\varnothing^{-1}(u), \varnothing^{-1}(v))$$

Simple! I have no idea what it means but it became known as the formula that killed Wall Street.

These credit default swaps and credit default obligations (insurance against loss) were developed on a mind-boggling scale. By June 2008:

> the International Swaps and Derivatives Association ... was estimating the total size of the market as $54 trillion, $54,000,000,000,000, close to the total GDP of the planet and many times more valuable than the total number of all the stocks and shares traded in the world.
>
> (Lanchester, 2010: 64)

Then the unforeseen (!) happened and the price of property began to fall. Negative equity was everywhere. Banks and their insurers went bust. It was time for you and me, in this country and the US, to step in and pick up the bill. The UK government bailed the banks out to the tune of £123.93 billion, and at its peak had liabilities for the banking crisis of £1.2 trillion, but the value of its stakes in the biggest banks has plummeted and the interest it is receiving on the loans is relatively small. The interest collected is smaller than the government pays on its debts taken out to refinance the banks.

Did this, at least, stop the rot? Not a bit of it.

In 2013 the figures are even more startling. World GDP is around $70 trillion and the market in interest rate derivatives some $310 trillion (Hutton, 2012: 30). The interest rate derivatives (bets on future interest rate movements) are bought and sold by traders and the benchmark rate at which banks can lend to each other is the Libor rate. Traders were cynically arranging to fix this rate on a regular basis, thereby amassing extra billions for their banks and large sums of money for their bonuses. Some of the banks found guilty and fined are Barclays, £290 million; RBS, £390 million; and UBS, £940 million. Fifteen other banks are under investigation.

Then there was the mis-selling of Insurance Protection Policies (IPPs) and the banks have been forced to set aside some £12 billion for compensation payments. HSBC were then fined £1.1 billion for allowing drugs barons to launder their money through the bank and Standard Chartered £415 million for money laundering with countries including Iran (figures from Stewart and Treanor, 2012: 34). A few people have had to resign with, alas, only a few millions to compensate them. Contrast this with the young woman in the UK riots of 2010 who picked up two left-footed trainers then threw them away and received ten months' imprisonment.

Even this did not put an end to the economic mismanagement of the banks. The banks in Cyprus had managed to run up balances eight times the national budget so when they crashed it was impossible to bail them out. For the first time the economics dictating the politics demanded that, in a move tantamount to theft, money be taken directly from bank accounts rather than be generated through taxes.

So what do these figures mean? It is easy to throw the terms billions and trillions around without a true measure of them. To try to get some sense of scale, ask yourself how long it would take to count to a trillion if you said a number a second.

The answer is 31,688 years, 279 days, 6 hours, 28 minutes and 32 seconds.[1]

The UK national debt is the total amount of money the British government (really you and I if you live in the UK) owes to the private sector and other purchasers of UK gilts. This debt stood at approximately £1.1 trillion at the end of December 2012 (Office for National Statistics publications, 23 January 2012). So if you handed over a £1 coin a second it would take more than 34,857 years to pay it off. Or, if you prefer to stack the coins one on top of the other, they will reach the moon nine times over. The total US debt is over $16 trillion. To pay that off at a dollar a second would take over 507,020 years (yes, over half a million years). If you want to be the centre of amazed friends, ask them how high a stack of dollar bills would need to be to pay off the US debt. It is worth having a guess yourself before reading on. The answer is it would need to stretch to the moon – wait for it – and back – wait some more – and there and back again and then halfway back once more. It would need to be 1,085,858 miles high.[2] Why bother with all these figures in a book on drama teaching? I hope it will become clear as we proceed.

The bankers are only part of the corrupt mentality that thrives in the UK. 'The bleak truth is that nearly all our key institutions have lost trust where they do not stand accused of outright corruption' (Freedland, 2012). Metropolitan police officers have been arrested on corruption charges in the Operation Elveden inquiry. The press has been blackened by the phone-hacking scandal. GlaxoSmithKline has paid out $3 billion after marketing antidepressants for treatment of children and teenagers even though the pills were not approved for that use (Freedland, 2012). Six of Britain's biggest water companies are using tax havens to avoid paying millions to the Treasury (*Guardian*, 10 November 2012). Gas companies have been accused of rigging prices to boost profits (*Guardian*, 13 November 2012). Horse meat has been passed off as beef. MPs are tarnished by the expenses scandal. Large global corporations like Starbucks, Google and Amazon pay little or no tax on profits of billions. There is no end to it. And you know who is paying the bill.

The UK coalition government's rhetoric is that welfare needs to be cut: it is the strivers versus the skivers. But the three years' benefit and tax credit cap will also affect (among the 'scroungers') '300,000 nurses, 150,000 teachers and 40,000 soldiers. The real term cuts will hit the poorest, lone parents, the disabled and women hardest, according to the government's own assessment … Just as 8,000 millionaires are about to get an average tax cut of over £107,000 …' (Milne, 2013a).

The government has fostered the illusion that welfare is claimed fraudulently whereas the government's own estimate is that it is '0.7% – or around £1 bn, compared to an estimated £70 bn worth of tax evasion [by big corporations]' (Milne, 2013a). Welfare payments will be cut by 14 per cent if a family on benefits has a spare bedroom (children under 16 of the same gender are expected to share a room and children under 10 must share regardless of gender). 'Camden council said that it would shortly be contacting 761 households, comprising 2,816 adults and children, because the coalition's benefit cap … will mean that they will be unable to afford their current accommodation or any other home in the south-east' (*Guardian*, 4 November 2012). Some will be sent 200 miles distant, away from extended families and friends to areas of high unemployment. Those at present in work will have to leave their jobs and will be unlikely to find any work in the new area. Other councils are planning to follow suit. Philip Hammond, the UK Defence Secretary, summed up the position of the neo-liberal when he said that the treasury should not cut military spending but the welfare budget. In other words, bombs not bread and homes. As Toynbee and Walker (2012) point out, Thatcher privatized the nationalized industries, Cameron would privatize the state itself. Laws have been passed that will lead to the privatization of education and the National Health Service. Hatcher (2011) shows with shocking clarity what will happen to education. Schools are being turned into academies, which means they are outside local authority control. Already academy head teachers can pay themselves higher salaries than the norm. They are often part of a chain of academies that must buy in services owned by the operating company. E-Act, a company that runs 11 academies, plans to run 250 in five years' time (Hatcher, 2011: 31). They are not for profit at the moment but watch this space. In the health service it is now clear that all work must be put out to private tender. This means hospitals' income will drop. Hospitals that fall into deficit can be privatized.

Do all these facts and figures matter? Yes – and no, not really. They will change today, tomorrow and the day after.[3] What is important is the change in mindset they represent: a culture that is the embodiment of the worship of the market, finance and the commodification of everything. There is a viciousness here, under the thinnest of pretended disguises. It is the voice of globalization. Tony Judt, in his last book, *Ill Fares the Land*, written while he was dying, gives a lucid accounting of this change in outlook.

> Something is profoundly wrong with the way we live today. For thirty years we have made a virtue out of the pursuit of material self-interest: indeed, this very pursuit now constitutes whatever remains of our sense of collective purpose. We know what things cost but have no idea what they are worth. We no longer ask of a judicial ruling or a legislative act: is it good? Is it fair? Is it right? Will it bring about a better society or a better world? Those used to be *the* political questions, even if they invited no easy answers. We must learn once again to pose them.

> Much of what appears 'natural' today dates from the 1980s: the obsession with wealth creation, the cult of privatization and the private sector, the growing disparity between rich and poor.
>
> (Judt, 2010: 1–2)

Even in 1982, when Margaret Thatcher's official think tank brought forward proposals to dismantle the welfare state, and presented them to the cabinet they provoked the 'nearest thing to a cabinet riot in the history of the Thatcher administration' (*Guardian*, 28 December 2012). This was a Conservative government and it was unthinkable then, let alone actable. Now it is being carried out with disparate and limited voices raised in protest up and down the country. As George Monbiot put it: 'A rightwing insurrection is usurping our democracy' (Monbiot, 2012). What I have outlined above is a picture of a completely corrupt society, played out in front of us while we have our heads down, eyes on our iPhones.

This is only a sketch of some of the major features of the neo-liberal agenda: the economic heart of globalization. It is largely limited to the UK and many countries are faring so much worse. I have not even mentioned child labour, famine, diseases that could be cured by cheap drugs that the big corporations will not license, species extinction, global warming, growing world population, mutual destruction from nuclear weapons ... you can finish the list. And I have not mentioned those Latin American countries that are, so far, bucking the neo-liberal trend: countries such as Ecuador, Bolivia, Venezuela, Brazil and Argentina. These countries have shown the lie of neo-liberal free market economic policies where the poor are made to pay for any crisis. In Ecuador, for example, they have 'cut poverty by a third and extreme poverty by 45%. Unemployment has been slashed, while social security, free health and education have been expanded – including free higher education, now a constitutional right – while outsourcing has been outlawed' (Milne, 2013b: 26). They have made the well-off pay their taxes (almost tripling government income in six years), regulated the banks, and extended nationalization. This is a working form of the third way but it is still capitalism – so watch for right-wing coups coming along, such as happened recently in Paraguay.

The crisis in culture

So how should we respond? It is certainly, as the late Stephane Hessell (2011) wrote, 'time for outrage'. This man had been captured along with thousands of other French soldiers in the Second World War, escaped, made his way to London, was parachuted back into France, joined the French Resistance, was captured again by the Gestapo, tortured, and sent to Buchenwald to be executed, narrowly missing death by switching identities with a dead man. While being transferred to Belsen he escaped again and after the war helped to draft the United Nations Declaration of Human Rights. He visited Gaza four times in his late 80s and early 90s and at the age of 94 went to support the Occupy Wall Street movement. His little pamphlet, *Time for Outrage*, written in his 90s, became an instant bestseller and has sold more than four million copies. His is a voice from a generation imbued with a sense of responsibility for the social good. He argues passionately that 'people must commit themselves in terms of their personal, individual human responsibility' (Hessell, 2011: 25).

And what are the personal, human responsibilities of artists today? There is a crisis in the arts. The arts and artists have become commodified along with everything else in the globalized economy. Danny Boyle's representation of British history at the opening ceremony of the 2012 Olympic Games was confined to the level of parody, where all was well with the National Health Service (with even Mary Poppins sailing down with a spoonful of medicine) and the butcher's apron of Britain's imperialist past conveniently avoided. No images, from the days of the Raj, of Indian mutineers tied across the mouths of cannon to be blasted into pieces. Likewise with his Bollywood *Slumdog Millionaire* (2008), in which India's desperate poverty is turned into a happy-ending all singing and dancing caper. We have arrived at a point in our culture where rewriting history and deliberately obfuscating huge social problems for the sake of entertainment have become acceptable, even expected.

Another example is the widespread accolade given to Tom Hooper's recent film adaptation of Victor Hugo's novel *Les Misérables*. The book is a scathing indictment of poverty in the French society of its time. Hugo supported the Paris Commune of 1870 and, at his own request, was buried in a pauper's coffin. Two million people attended his funeral. In the film version we have the degrading spectacle of the exploited poor of Paris paraded as thieves and all singing and dancing prostitutes, smeared with dirt but with their nails still immaculately manicured, with a Sweeney-Todd-and-his-wife type pub landlord providing supposed comic relief in snatches between hours of melodramatic attempts to pluck our heart strings. In the novel, Fantine, a young woman used by a young man and abandoned when she is pregnant, sells her hair, her two front teeth, and eventually herself in order to provide for her daughter. In the film her degradation is given relatively little screen time and ends with Anne Hathaway singing 'I dreamed a dream' with immaculate Hollywood pearl teeth. You cannot win an Oscar with two front teeth missing. It was a degrading spectacle. Once again, the distortion of history in order to satisfy mass audiences went largely uncriticized.

These are examples of popular entertainment by people who would regard themselves as artists but they reveal a culture at a stage of fundamental crisis. As Bond writes of theatre:

> English theatre [is] in a state of decline ... 'Don't look for a meaning. Watch the spectacle.' This is the ethos of contemporary English theatre. Its aim is to make money, its dramatic method is 'gift wrapping'. Its directing, acting, design – the mise-en-scene – and much of its writing is based on the mass culture of TV and Hollywood-Bollywood-Lollywood film.
>
> (Bond, 2012a)

My starting point was that 'the core business of drama' was not to respond to 'the worlds of corporation and government' nor to provide them with a workforce of 'designers, artists, musicians and performing arts consultants' who can 'empathise, think laterally, make fictional models of possible realities and communicate them to others', as I quoted O'Toole arguing earlier

(O'Toole, 2002). What then is the role of drama in this era of globalization? Bond suggests:

> Drama deals with society's madness and injustice and puts them [the audience] in their social situation. The audience enter into the situations, find themselves in them, because the situations are in the reality of their culture. The audience do this under the protection of fiction, in 'the suspension of belief.' But fiction is not an escape from reality but the human means of creating reality.
>
> (Bond, 2012b)

This is also the role of drama in schools no matter that the 'cop in the brain' tells us merely to prepare the pupils for Gove's examinations.

I have written about aspects of globalization in order to provide a background against which we can check if the forms of drama we are using in education and in applied theatre can measure up to the task of challenging 'society's madness and injustice'. This means a form of drama able to challenge the cultural mindset where everything appears 'normal' but is really insane.

In the following section I take a critical look at some of the publications on drama education that have come onto the market in recent years.

Notes

[1] http://wiki.answers.com/Q/How_long_is_1_trillion_seconds

[2] A dollar bill is 0.0043 inches (just over 0.1mm) thick, requiring nearly 233 dollar bills for a stack 1 inch high (http://wiki.answers.com/Q/What_is_the_thickness_of_a_dollar_bill). So, $0.0043 \times 16,000,000,000,000 = 68,800,000,000$ inches = 1,085,858.5858586 miles. Earth to the moon is 238,857 miles (www.universetoday.com/103206/what-is-the-distance-to-the-moon/), so 1,085,858.5858586 / 238,857 = 4.54606139179. (All mathematics checked by Dr Oylum Akkus Ispir and Alec Kimble.)

[3] As this book goes to press the total amount banks in the US and the UK have been fined for 'misconduct' stands at £130,000,000,000 and rising. No banker, to my knowledge, has gone to jail (Treanor, 2013).

Chapter 2

Responses and responsibilities

I think we've been through a period where too many people have been given to understand that if they have a problem, it's the government's job to cope with it. 'I have a problem, I'll get a grant.' 'I'm homeless, the government must house me.' They're casting their problem on society. And, you know, there is no such thing as society. There are individual men and women, and there are families. And no government can do anything except through people, and people must look to themselves first. It's our duty to look after ourselves ...

(Prime Minister Margaret Thatcher, talking to *Women's Own* magazine, 31 October 1987)

I have argued thus far that the neo-liberal dictatorship is the latest form of economics driving politics; politics being the way in which society is organized and whose interests are served by that organizing. While the primal drive to cooperate in the struggle for survival has been a key feature of our humanness from our earliest origins, since the Neolithic period humanity has split into classes, making society fundamentally unjust. To strive for a society based on meeting human needs rather than on profit through exploitation, has to be, for me at least, our human goal, and yet neo-liberalism is bent on destroying the essential striving of humans for a unified humanity. Art in this epoch must be focused on enabling the audience, spectator, reader, participant to glimpse the 'real' self-situation: the way in which every daily event is shaped in some way by these large social forces. It needs to open a space where we are faced with the 'actual' (what Bond calls 'imagining the real') and where our actions can be shaped by choices where fundamental questions of value can be fought out. Drama has a key role to play – in our theatres and, importantly, in our schools.[1]

In one of his earliest writings on drama Gavin Bolton wrote:

In teaching drama in schools my long-term aims are:

1) To help the student understand himself and the world he lives in
2) To help the student know how and when (and when *not*) to adapt to the world he lives in

3) To help the student gain understanding of and satisfaction from
the medium of drama

(Bolton, 1976: 1)[2]

I think it would be true to say that he never really moved far from this early statement. What he spent the rest of his teaching life searching for was the way best to achieve these aims, although he became much more gender generous as time went on! His drama teaching always centred on the self in society. This was also true for Dorothy Heathcote, whose drama was always on the cusp of the personal and the social. For both of them the personal out of the social context was never a key concern.

In the first of Bolton's aims there is an implication that through the experience of drama children will have the chance to develop an understanding of themselves as social beings. The 'when and when not to adapt' in aim 2 implies a deep analysis of the society in which the child is living and raises the key questions of the values we wish to live by. He continues in the same article:

What then are my goals? Put simply, I think I am always asking children the question, 'Can we set up some drama to help us find out how and why other people behave as they do, so that we can then reflect upon how we behave ourselves?'

(Bolton, 1976: 1)

The whole of this book revolves around trying to answer this question. Of key importance for me is what is meant by 'reflect', how to set up the reflecting process, and, of course, not focusing on individual psychology but searching for how social forces have entered us unbidden, unseen and unrecognized – but more of this later.

I had been teaching drama for ten years before I met Bolton and, through taking his Postgraduate Diploma in drama, for the first time began to have an induction into pedagogy and totally different ways of engaging students in drama. Up to this point I had been the pride and joy of my head teacher who would, with great care and reverence, bring visitors into the hall to observe my drama lessons. There they would find a darkened hall with carefully placed coloured spots giving off subtle lighting, the slow movement of Mendelssohn's Violin Concerto gently playing in the background and each child (11 year olds) carefully tending his or her dying rabbit in solitary silence. Tears would spring to their eyes (visitors and students) and, later, I would fend off the visitors' praise with feigned modesty. (Permission given to be sick at this point!)

Imagine my shock when, in the late 1960s, as well as meeting Bolton I first observed a demonstration lesson by Dorothy Heathcote in a local school (I lived and taught in the same area as Bolton and Heathcote). She was teaching a primary class and they were in role as poor farmers in early times, whose livelihood had been ruined by bad weather and having to spend too much time tending the lord's land. They had gathered at the door to their lord's manor to beg for his help, firm in the belief that he would help them; he was, after all, their benefactor. Dorothy Heathcote was in role as the gate-keeper (a go-between role and the first time I had seen it used). I still remember the stunned reaction of the children as the gate-keeper kept going to and fro with messages and it became clear that their lord was telling them that the small matter that their children were dying was their problem not his, and I was stunned also by the arguments and discussion it caused as they wondered about this. Why was this happening to them? What had they done to deserve this? Hadn't they always been loyal servants? What sort of person could he really be? And so on. I remember just as vividly my first experience of being in role with the other members of Bolton's Postgraduate Diploma course. We were in a retirement home and were going to be moved out for some reason. We were all suitably disturbed by this news and when I waved my stick at the owner of the home (Gavin Bolton in role) and told him off in a loud voice he turned on me with such an icy stare, telling me in a such an icy voice not to threaten him with my stick that afterwards, out of role, I hurried over to him to apologize, convinced that I had really upset him. He was suitably amused and explained to me, very patiently, that we had both been in role and that was what *being* in role meant. I got the message. So it was out with dying rabbits in darkened halls and in with queues of peasants with dying children being turned away from imposing front doors!

Much of my subsequent drama involved such moments of immediate destabilization that were aimed at opening reflective wonderings in the moment of the dramatic action, forcing a reassessment of the participants' take on the reality of the situation. As I write this several examples from thirty or more years ago come to mind. There was the drama where half the class were explorers, camping among old piles of stones in the jungle and suddenly realizing we were surrounded by the extremely hostile and armed people whose land it was (the other half of the class). I can still feel the moment when I, in role as one of the explorers, said 'Perhaps it's the same as if we found *them* camping in a church, lighting fires and spreading out food on the altar and going to the toilet behind the pews'. The explorers stopped in their tracks as they tried to work this out.

On another occasion Canadian teenagers wanted to do a drama about sex. I developed a play with them about disabled Vietnam veterans in convalescence supported by female volunteer nurses (it was the 1970s and the Vietnam War had not long ended). The female nurses had to move the men around so there was a lot of physical contact, all highly professional but nevertheless very intimate. The nurses, as part of the rehabilitation process, invited the veterans back to their apartments for a social visit. The veterans totally misread the invitation and both parties found themselves dealing with a highly embarrassing situation. It led into an unusually frank discussion about the problem of reading signs and dealing with sexual attraction. Again, it was the moment when the advance had to be dealt with that provided the shock. The drama had been devised so that the disabled veterans (teenagers playing the role of young men in their 20s) were looking to be seen as still attractive while the nurses were under strict instructions to be professional but of course may also have had submerged feelings of attraction. It meant neither was sure of the other's real feelings.

On another occasion I worked with a group of Canadian teenagers brought in from two different schools, observed by teachers on a university course. Clearly the pupils in these schools came from very different socio-economic backgrounds. This was revealed to me when the janitor came in to ask the person owning the Monte Carlo (a big North American car) to move it as it was blocking the drive. I turned to the teachers but a 17 year old sprang to his feet, apologizing, and went out to move his car. One half of the class were super-confident (the half the teenage car owner belonged to) and the other half were quite meek and mild, wanting to keep a low profile. We developed a drama where I asked who wanted to play the role of an important person and who wanted to be unimportant. The class divided almost exactly as I expected and hoped – the higher socio-economic group wanting to be the important people. I put them in role as leading scientists and doctors brought together from all over the world (easy to do in Canada) to join a research institute engaged in solving the question of whether or not there was life after death. The less important people all desperately needed money for their families and had all signed up to take part in the experiment, which would last a year. During this time these volunteers would be literally frozen to death so they showed no clinical signs of life. Large sums of money would be paid out monthly to the family dependents. After a year they were to be brought back to life to find out what had happened to them. I had prepared the 'unimportant' people to come back to life not knowing who they were, where they were, not recognizing anyone and so on. The experiment had clearly gone catastrophically wrong. I twice used the teachers observing the sessions in role as the press: the first time when some of them had got wind of the experiment and the scientists had to deal with very probing questions and the second time when the press got wind that something might have gone wrong. The super-confident teenagers had to fight for their professional lives. The moment when the volunteers were revived but did not come back to their same life as planned by these leading scientists caused a shock. This is, of course, only a potted outline of a drama that was spread out over five two-hour sessions. I heard from a mother of one of the students that they were still talking about it a year later – discussing the pros and cons of medical experiments, the ethics of taking advantage of low-income families, whether there was life after death and how you could ever find out, the positives and negatives of press investigations and so on.

I have briefly recounted these dramas, not as models of good practice but as examples of the sort of drama that many of us were developing from the influence of the early work of Dorothy Heathcote, work that Betty Jane Wagner called 'gut-level drama' (Wagner, 1974: 18). This is not the most useful way of describing it since, along with the shock, there was always a high level of reasoning provoked by the drama situation. In Bolton's outstanding history of classroom drama he points out that in the 1970s and '80s Heathcote moved away from 'Man in a Mess' drama[3] 'while other drama exponents, myself [Bolton] included, retain and develop it' (Bolton, 1998: 181). Heathcote moved more towards distancing modes of engagement.[4]

Interestingly, Heathcote describes it in the following way:

> What I'm trying to do here is to shake the reader out the conventional view of the curriculum, by using the principle of 'ostranenie' defined by Viktor Shklovsky as being 'that of making strange'. We very readily cease to 'see' the world we live in and become anaesthetised to its distinctive features. The arts permit us 'to reverse that process and to creatively deform the usual, the normal, and so to inculcate a new, childlike, non-jaded vision in us' … Art experiences insist upon a restructuring of ordinary perceptions of reality so that we end by seeing the world instead of numbly recognising it.
>
> (Heathcote, 1984a: 127–8)

This sounds very much like the central pursuit of this book – and it is – but by a different route, reaching a different destination. Bolton, commenting on the above, notices:

There is a Brechtian flavour in this, but whereas Heathcote's purpose was to invite the participants to 'see afresh', Brecht's purpose in defamiliarising was unremittingly social criticism. Heathcote, I believe, wanted her pupils continually to make judgements but not necessarily political ones.

(Bolton, 1998: 181)

Several areas immediately spring to mind. The main one is the interest in 'seeing the world instead of numbly recognizing it'. The focus on drama finding a form that can refocus our relationship to reality is key to the present book. Another is the claim that there was a Brechtian flavouring to Heathcote's work. This has been echoed in various places: in Muir (1996) and by Heathcote herself, in Heathcote and Fiala (1980): 'it [is] possible ... to demonstrate an artistic affinity between Dorothy Heathcote's approach, and Brecht's theory of Epic Theatre' (Heathcote and Fiala, 1980: 42). This is echoed in O'Toole, Stinson and Moore (2009): 'Brecht was a major influence on Heathcote's work, particularly in her use of distancing and framing techniques, as she and a number of her commentators have noted' (O'Toole *et al.*, 2009: 102). The most recent reference I have come across is in Eriksson: 'It is pertinent to an understanding of Heathcote's work to realize that all her foundational strategies are strategies of distancing' (Eriksson, 2011: 69).

Also central is Bolton's claim that Heathcote was not necessarily interested in political judgements nor in unremitting social criticism.[5] Brecht depoliticized is not Brecht at all but what remains is the distancing technique that will become a central concern of mine later and this is the point that Eriksson (2011) is making. However, Bolton's use of 'judgements' is interesting here and, to my reading, implies a sense of the highlighting of reasoning over the feeling-reasoning approach described in the drama examples above. Another thing to note is that Heathcote focuses on how drama can open up the 'curriculum' in a more productive way, signalling her move away from making a play and towards drama serving the curriculum. Her key contribution was the invention of Mantle of the Expert as a method of using drama to educate.

I remember Heathcote telling to teachers at a workshop the story of how her daughter came home from school one day to find things disturbed in the house – they had been burgled. Her daughter had phoned the police to report it in a fairly matter-of-fact way and the policewoman said with great urgency 'Get out of the house! Get out of the house!' Heathcote was making the point that the person at a distance from the event could get a much clearer picture of what was happening than the person in the event: the burglar might still be upstairs. This could be extended to drama events where, for example, the children want to be in a fire, a 'raging inferno' scenario, which would mean children dodging falling timbers, choking to death from the smoke, and doing other things that would be great fun instead of ordinary lessons. But for Heathcote the students could get closer to experiencing a fire in a school if their role was framed from a perspective outside the event itself. In an example I witnessed on one of Heathcote's in-service courses for teachers, the fire happened to be in a boarding school. The students were in role as teachers sifting through the wreckage to see if they could find any of the dead pupils' belongings to pass on to the parents. They were not in the fire at all but approaching it from a frame distance.

Heathcote was undoubtedly the driving force and inspiration for a whole new way of using drama in schools. In the 1950s and '60s she ploughed her own furrow, an independent contemporary of Peter Slade and Brian Way, developing teacher in role and 'living through' drama, developing drama events where the pupils were given the opportunity to restructure 'the ordinary perceptions of reality'. In the 1970s and '80s, as Bolton describes above, she moved away from this direct experiencing from within the event to increasingly valuing how perception could be sharpened from outside the event, engaging with it from a different perspective. This was when several of those who became leading figures in the drama education world began to find their own voices. Cecily O'Neill, who at one stage studied with Bolton, developed her own version of process drama written up in the very useful *Drama Worlds* (O'Neill, 1995). Jonothan Neelands developed his own approach that worked through versions of whole-group drama (Neelands, 1984) to his conventions approach (Neelands and Goode, 2000).

Bolton remained closest to Heathcote's original 'Man in a Mess', although developing it in his own way:

> I have to a large extent been responsible for a re-interpretation of Heathcote's methodology that has taken 'Living through' Drama in a direction never intended by her and perhaps, from her point of view, off-target, if not misguided.
>
> (Bolton, 1998: 217)

Bolton developed Slade's interest in child play into new pathways. He maintained the immediacy of 'being' another, demonstrated in children's make-believe play, but in 'play'/a play that was shaped by the components of drama as an art form. It is interesting that he quotes Peter Millward's work as an example of this 'being' in role:

Teacher	Can you imagine that each of you ... [is] a person who lives in a little village by a volcano, all right? And I'm a stranger and I'm coming to talk to you. All right?
All	Mmm
Teacher	Can you do that from this moment? Stop being yourselves for a moment, well, be yourselves ... but [laughter] be yourselves in this village.

(Bolton, 2010b: 12)

This 'being' rather than 'pretending' was key to Bolton's approach: 'I am making it happen. It is happening to me', to which Cecily O'Neill added 'I am watching this happening to me' (O'Neill, 1995: 125). 'Being' in two worlds at once Bolton called *metaxis*, using the term introduced by Augusto Boal. This immediacy is exemplified in the account of his own process drama described in detail in *Acting in Classroom Drama* (Bolton, 2010b: 6–11). In this example, part of a drama structure to open up Arthur Miller's *The Crucible*, the young people, some of whom were seen dancing naked in the wood the previous evening, are faced with a direct experience. In the previous stage of the structure they have written on a piece of paper 'GUILTY' or 'INNOCENT' to denote whether or not they danced naked in the woods. In the next stage of the drama, as Bolton recounts:

> In my role [as pastor] I then give them [all the families, parents and children gathered in the chapel] the news of sacrilegious behaviour in the woods. I warn them of the wrath of God and speak of dire punishment. I then invite each 'child' in turn to come forward, place a hand on the Bible (it has obviously to be *not* a Bible, of course – this is Drama) and say after me: 'My soul is pure'.
>
> (Bolton, 2010b: 9–10)

It cannot get much more direct than this. But as Heathcote developed her distancing approach, particularly in Mantle of the Expert, the role was always 'conducted with a cool eye of "this is how it was for *them*" or "this is how it would be for *them*"; never "this is happening to us *now*"' (Bolton, 1998: 241). And again, Heathcote ploughs her own furrow:

> Heathcote unambiguously adopts the position of an *educationist* harnessing the potential of drama, setting herself apart from her contemporary drama specialists who see drama as an important area of a person's education – in competition with other curriculum

subjects. Whereas their attention necessarily is on drama, hers is on the curriculum and whatever is to be taught determines the kind of fiction that will be needed. However, and this is critical to the approach, the *fictional starting point will rarely be that of the matter being studied*. Thus, if we take examples from Heathcote (1995), the American students studying 'Watergate' were in role as 'people running a museum'; for the topic of an 'aircrash' the pupils were in role as 'radio engineers'; for a study of China, the roles were running a hotel management training school.

(Bolton, 1998: 241)

Heathcote herself describes this turn away from drama *per se* in the following words:

Finally, having spent a long time wondering why I have for years been irritated by the cry of 'let's have more drama in our schools', I now realize why I always wanted to say, don't lobby for dramatics, lobby for better learning!

(Heathcote, 1984b: 169)

This Mantle of the Expert work has now been very successfully developed by Luke Abbott and his co-workers, as evidenced in their impressively productive website, Mantle of the Expert.com.

'Restructuring ... ordinary perceptions of reality' and the problem of ideology

Clearly Bolton and Heathcote were both developing drama that was concerned with students re-cognizing their world and their relationship to it. This is the world I have tried to outline in the Introduction. In dealing with the problem of re-cognizing society, Bolton and Heathcote are dealing with the same problems faced by European playwrights from Ibsen to Brecht and Bond. However the immediate engagement, the 'being' in role of Bolton, I suggest, is qualitatively different to the distancing of Heathcote. This Brechtian distancing influence, or flavour, I argue, has largely come to dominate much of drama education, particularly in the UK, not necessarily in a political sense but in the way the role is framed in relation to the event. This qualitative difference is also to be found in the way Bond places the audience compared with Brecht. To repeat part of an earlier quotation: 'Drama deals with society's madness and injustice and puts them [the audience] in their social situation. The audience *enter into the situations, find themselves in them*, because the situations are in the reality of their culture' (Bond, 2012b, emphasis added).

And again: 'What I try to do in my plays is to speak directly to every individual to make them responsible for their own assessment and involvement in what is being shown – from the individual into the general – not to try and impose a general concept' (Bond, 2004).

With Brecht the audience stays outside the situation, in a relationship to the events where they have, or rather are manipulated into having, the moral high ground, 'thinking above the stream' (Brecht: 1978: 44). In Bond's plays 'The audience are shown their site by being placed in it – not, as in Brecht, outside it' (Bond, 2000: 11): imagination seeking reason, with the audience up to their necks *in* the stream, rather than the audience employing reason and criticism from outside the event. However, this would seem to compound the problem and take us back to the moment when Heathcote and Brecht recognized the limitations of seeing clearly while in the middle of the mess.[6] All of this is examined in Part Three.

I have argued elsewhere that in order to begin to develop form in drama we need to return to the early Heathcote and the later Bolton (Davis, 2005: 174). It is the immediate engagement with role that comes nearer to Bond's approach, than does distancing from the event, which has a Brechtian flavour. But why does this matter? On the face of it, it would seem to make sense to get outside the event to take a closer look at it.

It may be necessary to take a preliminary look at the problem of ideology even though I discuss it later. Why are we so likely to have something stare us in the face and not recognize it but ignore it? As a species we seem to have this ability to imagine a reality that is clearly other than it is. Saul (1997) gives an example of how people ignore evidence staring them in the face. Before Benjamin Franklin began to think about lightning, people saw it as a supernatural phenomenon. They stored gunpowder in churches for divine protection and church bells were rung during storms to ward off bad spirits. 'Between 1750 and 1784, lighting struck 386 German churches, killing 103 bell ringers. In 1767 lightning struck a Venetian church whose vaults were filled with gunpowder. The explosion killed 3,000 people' (Saul, 1997: 167). People could not be blamed for not yet understanding the science of thunderstorms, however, there seems to be some evidence for not continuing to believe churches would be safe places to store gunpowder.

Go into any bookshop and books jump off the shelves into our arms demanding that we open our eyes to what is happening all around us. Monbiot's *Captive State: The corporate takeover of Britain* (2000) shows how companies have come to dominate key government ministries, how planning permission is bought and sold, how big business is taking over the food chain. In *The Best Democracy Money Can Buy* (2002) Palast, an investigative journalist, unearths all the documentary evidence you will ever want to see about how an alliance of corrupt politicians, their fixers, criminals and idiot academics are making the world safe for international capital. Franken's *Lies and the Lying Liars Who Tell Them: A fair and balanced look at the right* (2003) takes the Bush administration apart along with its allies in Fox News. Pilger's *The New Rulers of the World* (2002) sets out to break the silence about the new world order, its purposes and effects in developing a globalization of poverty for the mass of the people in the world. Chomsky's *Hope and Prospects* (2011) is a devastating critique of aspects of globalization. Milne's *The Revenge of History: The battle for the 21st Century* (2012) looks at how a neo-liberal economic order has brought the world to its knees. And these are just a few examples.

On the one hand, what is going on in the world is as clear as daylight and, on the other, our actions are not based on an understanding of the larger picture. As with Brecht, these books place us above the stream where our own moral and ethical agenda is left intact and we look at the corrupt world through the eyes of reason. But the problem is in us. Although these books are enormously useful guides to the world we inhabit, when reading them we are somehow above that world rather than complicit in it and an essential part of its ability to function. Using reason alone is, to paraphrase Bond, like asking a blind man to open his eyes wider in order to see. We remain within, and work with, the ideology we are trying to recognize.

This whole area and these broad statements need much more justification and I consider them in detail in Part Three.

For now, it will suffice to build a platform for my thesis to examine recent trends in drama in education, to justify the claim that reflective modes have dominated and examine whether or not there have been new developments in form that have taken us out of that siding. I recognize that, early on, Heathcote also was responsible for introducing distancing devices but her work moved into mainstream curriculum education rather than remaining with 'Man in a Mess' and process drama. My main argument is that Jonothan Neelands's conventions forms have been one of the major influences to spread distancing approaches, keeping us in the siding and, in fact, taking us into reverse.

Jonothan Neelands and conventions drama

I remember first hearing Dorothy Heathcote use the word 'convention' in relation to drama in the late 1960s. It seemed an alien word until I realized that it meant a customary way of doing something that children would recognize, such as looking at a picture in a gallery or watching a video clip played as many times as needed. She developed her conventions as a way of engaging students with the material they were studying from a frame perspective that would lead into the drama they were making. She eventually wrote these up in her now-famous 'Signs and Portents' (Heathcote, 1984b).[7] Neelands developed his later, for a different purpose, as he identifies below, and he wrote this up in Neelands (1990) and Neelands and Goode (2000).

In Peter O'Connor's useful collection of Neelands's writings (O'Connor, 2010), Neelands explains how his set of conventions were inspired by Heathcote's but:

> We [they were developed in conjunction with Tony Goode and Warwick Dobson] were interested in a much wider set of conventions [than Heathcote's] that did not assume the Stanislavskian 'living through' mode associated with the DiE and Process Drama traditions. In particular, we were interested in taking a more Brechtian or epic realist approach to drama. To use conventions to puncture the illusion of 'reality' in process drama and to make the contents of drama strange rather than to make it familiar.
>
> (O'Connor, 2010: xviii)

Neelands here claims his approach is Brechtian and again, later, O'Connor quotes Neelands as claiming 'All *Structuring Drama Work* conventions are Brechtian in the sense that they disrupt realism and make strange' (Neelands in O'Connor, 2010: 4).

Neelands mounts an all-out attack on the form of process drama advocated by Bolton and the early Heathcote in language reminiscent of the criticisms voiced by Hornbrook, Abbs and Ross in the 1980s. (And, incidentally, on the form of drama I describe in the next section.)

> Spending four hours or more in the classroom 'building investment' and 'belief' in an imagined character and situation prior to an 'authentic' role-play is, in fact, a mythologised dilution of the working practices of Stanisalvski, Michael Chekov and their followers.
>
> (Neelands, 2006: 143)

He does this while misrepresenting it, as those early attackers did.

> The participants in process drama, like Stanislavski's actors, are 'living through' the given circumstances of the imagined situation 'as-if' these events were actually occurring to them; they are 'being' in role, or character. In process drama, there is a 'consensus' that all those present exist, temporarily, within the immediate dramatic world. They are bound to its parameters of space and time rather than their own actualities. In 'process drama' we can be denied any social space, outside of the bounds of the drama world, in which to comment and reflect from within our own parameters of existence and difference … it is a psychological and private mode of learning based on how we feel as a result of our drama experiences.
>
> (Neelands, 2000: 102)

Bolton replies to all these criticisms, as they were originally voiced by Hornbrook *et al.*, in Davis (2010: 121–51) and the replies will not be repeated in detail here. Suffice it to point to key areas that are misrepresented.

Bolton's aim was precisely to avoid the above total immersion in an experience, while absolutely maintaining the strength of the experience. This is why, although he describes it as 'being' in role, he incorporates the notion of *metaxis* into his work: being in two worlds at once. He aims to have the possibility of reflection built into the experience without relinquishing the strength and immediacy of that experience. This is the area that I consider key to process drama work and one that needs to be maintained and built on in any attempt to develop the form of that work.

Also, to term all 'living through' modes Stanislavskian is open to question. Certainly, Bolton finds connections between Stanislavski and Slade and Way (see Bolton, 1998: 126–50) but not to his own work (see below). And although Neelands, above, is already acknowledging Heathcote's move to distancing, there could be an implication that her early work was also influenced by Stanislavski. However, she never saw herself in that tradition. She distances herself from Stanislavski, whose approach focused on the subjective relationship of the actor with the role. As we see in the monograph written with Oliver Fiala, 'she stands apart from the majority of drama practitioners who ally their educational ideas with Stanislavskian theatrical ideas' (Heathcote and Fiala, 1980: 37). Neither would O'Neill see herself as a Stanislavskian: she recognizes that, 'a degree of distance is required in the roles with which the participants are endowed' (O'Neill, 1995: 125).

Bolton too would not see himself as a Stanislavskian. Rather he makes very clear that the personal, subjective, psychological approach that more properly belongs to Stanislavski has nothing to do with his own approach to creating drama, which in his latest formulation he terms 'making':

> We can no longer characterise drama that is not specifically prepared for an audience as a 'self-expressive', 'personal', 'private', 'individual', and 'subjective' process – all the characteristics that used also to be thought to belong to child make-believe. Certainly both child play and 'living through' drama are examples of 'making', but I am proposing that the principal determinants are not to be found in the egocentric list in the above sentence but in directions that have not previously been considered.
>
> (Bolton, 1998: 271)

He goes on to list four ways in which 'making' drama is cultural rather than just personal. It is the social/personal he is interested in rather than the Stanislavskian personal in the social. Neelands is obviously at liberty to challenge Bolton here – but not to ignore his detailed analysis of classroom drama and just make claims with no counter-argument.

Neelands (in O'Connor, 2010: 107) repeats the claims made in the 1980s against process drama, that pupils exist on a diet of the same sort of whole-class drama and learn nothing about the art form: the old claim that in process drama there is no progression. I quoted Bolton above, writing in 1976, where he clearly states that one of his fundamental aims is to help the students get better at doing drama and understanding how the art form works. By 1992 he is writing in very direct language that he has become 'so alienated' by the separation implied by learning *in* drama (learning theatre arts skills) and learning *through* drama (drama that provides possibilities of new ways of understanding) that he regards it as totally erroneous to try to divorce the two. Correctly, in my view, he argues that form and content cannot be separated in this way. This is a position which is echoed by Fleming in many places, not least in *Teaching Drama in Primary and Secondary Schools: An integrated approach* (2001).

Neelands confirms his allegiance to Brecht in the following words:

> In the presentational mode of theatre-making associated with Brecht ... experience is shown rather than lived. We demonstrate through dramatic representations, or depictions, the way the world is and how it works. We illustrate, rather than illude, our understanding of human behaviour and experience. In the presentational mode,

there **must** be an audience who respond as themselves to what is being demonstrated and who are aware that the 'dramatic world' is nothing more and nothing less than an imaginary construction: a hermeneutic that needs constantly testing and modifying against our existing (or becoming) imaginaries of the world. Learning in the presentational mode is through public discussion, comment and the voicing of different conceptions of the world; it is sociological and public, based on what is actually said and done rather than on what is 'felt' or 'experienced'. The purpose of Brecht's theatre was to show the world, and therefore the circumstances of the drama world, as changeable and to show that the outcomes of the drama may well be predictable according to political principles and the logic of human history. It is a theatre of knowing, rather than a theatre of cathartic understanding.

(Neelands, 2000: 102)

There is no room for doubt that Neelands's central contribution to form in drama education is firmly in a Brechtian tradition, at least in his own eyes. The above quotation contains pretty well all the main areas that Bond has criticized in Brecht's work since the 1960s. Bond argues for a form of drama where reflection begins in the immediacy of the experience.[8] Responding as spectators to the experience, as Neelands advocates above, forces us to reason from within our own ideological framework. Bond's drama form seeks ways to subvert our ideological outlook and prompt us to connect with our sense of what is just and unjust formed early in our lives and then to consider why we live in a society that forces injustice on us and what our own responsibilities are. Again, all this is substantiated in Part Three. Suffice it to claim here that far from this Brechtian distancing mode 'Putting living reality in the hands of living people' (Neelands, 2000: 103), which, in one sense, it cannot avoid doing, it rather puts ideologized reality in the hands of ideologized people.

Neelands's two editions of *Structuring Drama Work* have been reprinted 27 times at the last count. This must make it the widest-selling book on drama education internationally and, along with his other writings, makes Neelands one of the most influential writers in this field. Neelands himself promotes this view when he states that:

In England we have been developing a way of working in drama that has sought to include both the presentational and representational modes. This way is often referred to as the 'conventions' approach, because it employs a wide range of 'means' drawn from both the representational and presentational traditions. Following Brecht's advice we have sought to make lively use of all means.[9]

(Neelands, 2000: 102–3)

This level of influence is germane to my thesis that it needs to be explored, and areas resisted.

Much more could be examined in Neelands's writings but it will have to suffice to point to one more worrying area. He writes of the need for the drama teacher to be a censor who should have no 'concerns about either banning or confounding prejudicial images and characteristics' (Neelands, 1997: 54). Goodbye to innocent Desdemona being murdered by her black husband and the Jewish Merchant being humiliated by the court in Venice. Instead the drama teacher should, according to Neelands, promote 'values such as tolerance, justice, compassion, respect for others', which 'will be influenced by his/her own moral and political ideologies' (Neelands and Goode, 2000: 109). This is the stuff of ideology. Whose tolerance, justice, compassion are we talking about: the justice to sentence a young man to 35 years' imprisonment for revealing how the state spies on us all?; the compassion to tolerate begging in the streets?; and so on. And again, he describes drama as a vehicle to 'develop central societal concepts such as democracy, justice and freedom' (Neelands, 1992: 37). What happened to Bolton's 'To help the student know how and when (and when *not*) to adapt to the world he lives in' quoted earlier? The 'when *not* to' is of key importance.

Both Neelands and O'Connor point to the frustration they feel at the formulaic way in which the conventions approach has been used to give structure to drama lessons. It is therefore rather puzzling that Neelands and Goode did not take the opportunity of the second edition to address this. Rather than tackling this central problem they added some 24 extra conventions and edited out the two examples of process dramas in the first edition. These had at least provided a minimal demonstration of how the conventions could be used as structures in a process drama rather than as stand-alone techniques.

In the next section I take a wider look at a sample of drama publications to see if there are any instances of development in drama forms and to examine how widespread the influence of distancing modes has been. I am conscious that all drama teachers tend to be passionate about their subject and hold a deep conviction of its value to the development of their students. Because of this I have found it somewhat difficult to decide what stance to take in the next section. At a time when drama is under attack I do not want to take on only the role of critic, although my starting point in this publication is to take a long hard look at how we are measuring up to the crucial stage we, as artist educators, have reached in our social development. Nor do I want to appear as a reviewer of the writings of others, although this may be part of what I want to achieve. I suppose it is a mixture of the above, with the caveat that I aim to put my own practice under the same critical scrutiny and review in the third part of this book. I hope that this will leaven the critical voice above and what may appear hereafter, as I aim to direct the same voice towards my own work. I suppose I am asking us all to take a long hard look at what we are doing in the social context of neo-liberal globalization where everything is being commodified, including ourselves.

A wider view

I start with Helen Nicholson's *Theatre, Education and Performance* (2011). Her book covers an impressive range of sources and raises the sorts of questions I am concerned with here. In a key section of the book she argues that the major challenge facing theatre makers and educators is the development of a globalized economy. She sets out to investigate which contemporary drama/theatre practices are responding to the challenges young people face in such a world.

She notes the shift away from the nineteenth- and twentieth-century approaches of seeing creativity as an antidote to 'the dehumanising effects of industrial labour' (Nicholson, 2011: 92) and how there is now a move to link creativity with the economy. She usefully quotes Massey (2005) who points out that capital is free to travel round the world in search of profit but the poor and unskilled in search of work, travelling across the same borders, are tracked down by sniffer dogs. Nicholson sets out both sides of the argument for educators – on the one hand the need to help young people to benefit and survive in a globalized world by enabling them to develop the flexibility required in an era of innovation and change, and on the other the need to 'find a secure set of pedagogic principles and social values' (Nicholson, 2011: 97) to resist this individualized route to supporting consumerism and the commodification of everything. As a chief advocate of the former approach she cites Ken Robinson's book *Out of Our Mind: Learning to be creative* (2001). She comments 'Robinson's emphasis on creativity in education ... represents a new way of thinking in which creativity is not an expression of personal fulfilment, nor a Morrisonian socialist utopia, but a commercially exploitable and marketable commodity'

(Nicholson, 2011: 94). (To my mind this is Robinson in his most reactionary and degenerative mode.)

Nicholson, without being as direct as I am, certainly argues against selling out to the market. She condemns the UK Government's Creative Partnerships scheme and refers to their website definition of creativity as a 'corporate statement of belief' and 'an instrumental justification for creativity which links "today's employers" [quoting from the website] with global capitalism' and implicitly connects Robinson to the same critique.

She sets out an enjoyable satire of what an educational approach to creativity for the market would look like if such an approach were followed by drama teachers:

> We might set an assignment that asks young people to create a piece of theatre that would attract the biggest audiences (or largest number of participants). It should be branded and exportable. Extra points would be awarded for merchandise opportunities – mugs, DVDs or pet accessories for example – might attract a special bonus. The show should either appeal to the exclusive metropolitan classes or to a mass market. A franchise might be established for participatory work in the corporate or charitable sectors, and games and activities would be subject to copyright ... The assessment might include an interview to ascertain which person had been most creative. Students would be encouraged to compete, perhaps by denigrating the contribution of the teammates (rather like the popular reality TV show *The Apprentice* in which competitors battle for a highly paid job with a well-known business personality).
>
> (Nicholson, 2011: 95)

She gathers a range of sources to support the need to find in what ways 'theatre education might continue to provide a voice of opposition to the commodification of culture and childhood' (Nicholson, 2011: 99). She usefully states that the 'debate turns on how imagination is conceptualized and understood' and argues that 'In contemporary social life the imagination has become a commodified social practice which transcends national boundaries' (99).

In a section headed 'Dramatizing the imagination ...' we seem to be heading into interesting territory, germane to the concerns of this book, where Nicholson draws on Féral's writing that theatre creates a gap between everyday space where there is usually no disjuncture between signs and their meanings and the representational space where things might be perceived differently (Nicholson, 2011: 105). This all sounds very interesting and relevant to Bond's pursuit but then Nicholson draws on examples that use different performance spaces to undo the corrupted imagination by moving from conventional theatre spaces and into 'vernacular' spaces. It is the disruption caused by the different spaces in which the theatre is experienced that is intended to provide the impetus to new ways of seeing. This is disappointing. Many of the concerns of this book had been raised and a human-centred approach pursued, but the way in which the gap could be used remains general. The theatre 'text' itself does not seem as important as the location in which images are experienced so that performance theory seems to come to the fore. The main focus of the rest of her book is made up of examples of theatre used in this way.

She relates an example from Everyday Theatre in New Zealand where family violence is explored as if 'the family were characters in an arcade game' to 'provide a protective aesthetic frame through which the students interpreted the issues' (115). Conventions seem to have been used to encourage this reflection, such as freezing the action, thought tracking, replaying moments of the action and so on. This seems to me to be a fairly 'conventional' way of distancing to aid reflective discussion.

In another example she describes work on *The Tempest* with third-generation British Asians living in Southall, London, to explore their notions of national identity. The pupils explored the play in a series of workshops that Nicholson does not describe in detail but the project ends with key speeches from the play, recorded on individual MP3 players, which audience members would listen to at key points on a route around Southall chosen by the pupils.

In Japan, Nicholson and three of her students worked with children on the theme of 'Citizenship: Our narratives'. The performance was a promenade one where the 'children led the adults through the building, inviting them into different spaces and, at one stage, shouting very loudly at the audience' (Nicholson, 2011: 172) (a reference to a previous experience when it had proved almost impossible to get the children to speak at all).

Another example describes an interesting project funded by the Wellcome Trust where performance artist Mark Storer and educationalist Anna Ledgard spent several months working with children in a hospital's dialysis unit. The performance took place in the Unicorn Theatre. 'The performance was an installation, taking place not in a conventional auditorium, but it took the form of a journey through the backstage space, lifts, scene docks and dressing rooms before opening out onto the wide open space of the closed-in stage' (187). The performance explores a family's story of coming to terms with their child's kidney failure, haunted by the spectre of his death, and different locations were used as home, hospital, and so on. Nicholson writes about the effect on her as 'intensely poetic … most of all I shall remember the feelings I had, and in particular that deep and familiar pull right in the middle of my chest that is reserved for only the most intense of life's experiences and for which there are no words' (188).

All the above appear to be interesting examples of inventive drama work and seem to be exploring the effects brought about by the choice of location causing a disruption of the expected relation of signs and meanings. But I could not see any evidence of the drama form having helped the participants find society in themselves (to paraphrase Bond). I could see, in the last example above, that Nicholson had been profoundly moved by the evocations from the different locations but not how she came to realize that the society in her was busy killing children with kidney failure through the destruction of the health service. I am willing to be convinced that I am missing what is staring me in the face but there was so little detail of the working with young people that it was difficult to form a clearer picture. I remain unconvinced that this is the productive development in form which she describes as being 'at the cutting edge of contemporary theatre' (Nicholson, 2011: 6). Edward Bond critiques this approach in the Foreword to Nicholson's monograph *Theatre and Education* where she covers similar ground to the above: 'It is an illusion to suppose that aesthetic events instigate moral or rational imperatives' (Bond, 2009: x).

Rather than cover this ground again suffice it to remark that in her latter publication, *Theatre and Education*, Nicholson again promotes the notion of there being an exciting new form for drama to found in the dislocation produced by a series of images in site-specific locations. An example she uses is of a project called *Boychild*, on 'bioethical issues of maleness and masculinity' (Nicholson, 2009: 65). It took place in the disused Admiralty Underwater Weapons building in Portland on Father's Day. After they had listened on a headset to the voice of the former caretaker reminiscing about his work and life:

> A small boy beckoned us into the building, taking us on a journey that would trace life from birth to old age and death. Walking along the corridors, peeping into some rooms and lingering in others was an intense experience. In one room a teenage boy lay in his pyjamas on a beautifully lit mound of unwashed potatoes,

carefully turning over one at a time as a recorded poem was played that described the boys' experiences of their bodies in puberty:

> Why do men's hearts give out before women's?
> I dig my hands into the earth, fingers curl around unfamiliar forms.
> As my body sprouts I am an oddly shaped potato.
>
> (Nicholson, 2009: 66)

Nicholson is drawing on Paul Ricoeur's notion that there are different roles for the imagination: a creative utopian one and one that preserves the social order. 'A productive imagination can emerge when the utopian imagination that looks forward to create the future is in dialogue with the ideological symbols of the past' (50). Such a disjuncture occurs when the two collide as in the above example. I am afraid I remain unconvinced by this argument. I cannot recognize anything in the above installation that would prevent the viewer perceiving the event through their ideologized eyes. It is the minute attention that Bond gives to evoking a creative imagination that is at the centre of his work and that will need to be set against the above in Part Three. Again, I cannot see how representations 'such as site specific performances, live art, installation and autobiographical performance' are 'at the cutting edge of contemporary theatre making' (46).

The theatre world that Nicholson describes is part of the one that Lehmann introduces in his *Postdramatic Theatre* (2006). This is a theatre that has broken with all forms where dialogue is dominant including Brechtian theatre. He traces its origins in Performance Theory from the 1960s onwards but describes a neo-realist wave in German theatre in the 1990s. In the introduction, one of these 'happenings' (I cannot see how it can be called drama in any way that makes sense) is described. The members of the audience enter the performance space in semi-darkness and are invited to reach through holes of large vertical cylinders only to find themselves feeling naked performers. They are caught red-handed when the tubes rise in the air and the 'audience' find themselves being glared at by the performers, now fully clothed and masked. Other moments include a 'performer speaking a monologue from Oscar Wilde while eating dog food out of a can; the same performer … singing "You make me feel like a natural woman" while dressed in a 17th-century shepherdess outfit with the front panel missing (thus exposing his genitals); and another performer having cake stuffed up his bum' (Jürs-Munby, 2006: 4). This cannot be directly related back to life in the society I have described. It is private and works in an individual rather than a social way. It works for a shock response but one that cannot easily be related to the everyday life of the 'audience'. Drama needs to be able to involve us in such a way that we meet ourselves giving us the possibility of reworking the ideology that has entered us: the possibility of glimpsing how society has corrupted us. This is the *metaxis* effect that Bolton seeks to evoke through students *being* in the drama and Bond seeks to effect in the audience through the drama structures he employs.

An even wider view

When I came to survey the books on using drama for some sort of educational/developmental purpose, published over the last 13 years or so, what surprised me was how many there have been. In the time available to write this book it has been impossible to read them all, but I have tried to take a cross-section of publications.[10] My main interest is drama in education but I have dipped into Applied Theatre and Theatre in Education (I am not one of those who see process drama as a branch of Applied Theatre). I accept, therefore, that my research provides no more than a snapshot and would be more than happy to have my conclusions proved to be wrong. My priorities were to find out if there have been major developments in form in this period; to see if I could confirm the suspicion that a conventions approach is widespread; to determine to what extent a Brechtian influence (distancing mode) predominates; to examine how ideology is being tackled; and to see if the work of Edward Bond is appearing as an influence.

This proved unexpectedly elusive. There was no simple way to check against the categories above. For example, in the thirty or so books surveyed in this present section alone, there was no in-depth exploration of the central problem of ideology, which would seem to me a *sine qua non* for anyone writing about the role and purpose of contemporary drama. There were occasional references to the area of ideology. For example, Prendergast and Saxton (2009) cite from an article by Chinyowa:

> Theatre for development aims to interrogate the structures of fixed reality in order to 'un-fix' them. It attempts to subvert the dominant ideology, to re-order the received unities of time, space and character through fictional reconstruction of those unities.
>
> (Chinyowa, 2007: 37)

However, this seems to me to do no more than suggest that restructuring events into dramatic form is enough to destabilize established ideological perceptions. I think the whole question is much more complicated than this, as I attempt to explore later.

Apart from the postdramatic examples referred to above, Carroll *et al.* (2006) also offer a development of drama form. They present an interesting exploration of drama interacting with the digital revolution. They aim for a live form but enriched by technology (Carroll *et al.*, 2006: xvi) to produce a hybrid form that they call 'situated role'. They claim this shares all the features of process drama 'but is situated in a dramatically mediated "reality" that augments the imagined context in a classroom' (3) and that this hybrid new form can 'augment what can be achieved by imagination alone' (12). The weakness in this argument, for me, is that it does not do enough to isolate what makes live drama a unique art form. They 'argue drama can and does happen on stage, on screen, in real and virtual spaces and in a mixture of all these' (53). This seems to me to mix the dramatic with live drama/ theatre. The unique dimension of live theatre is that the participant/audience is present at an enactment of a live event, or involved in enacting it, that it is not mediated through the eye of the director or the manipulator of the media effects. There is the chance to perceive what is happening in 'reality' without any enhanced aid to seeing. The media effects are likely anyway to distance the participants/audience in the ways described above.

In the publications reviewed, Edward Bond's name is mentioned a few times with a quotation or two but there is no serious attempt to analyse what is new in the way his plays are formed. The exceptions here are John Doona's books *Drama Lessons for the Primary School Year* (2013a) and *Secondary Drama* (2013b) and Chris Cooper's chapter on 'The performer in TIE' in Jackson and Vine (2013). Doona has collaborated with Bond over a number of years and in his books attempts to relate Bond's work to creative drama. Chris Cooper has worked closely with Bond for the last 18 years or so and in this chapter gives a clear exposition of the demands of Bondian theatre on the actor. Another key contribution to understanding Bondian theatre has been Kostas Amoiropoulos's PhD (2013). In this study he isolates the key components of Bond's theatre that would be needed in process drama. However, in the other publications I could find no serious attempt to tackle the central problem that has focused Bond's mind over the last fifty years or so: how to open a window to enable the audience to make a direct connection between their own lives and responsibilities and the world of which they are a part without seeing the world through the opaque lens of ideology; offering the audience the opportunity to create their own humanness in this process. The fact that none of the books surveyed attempted this is an extraordinary situation in itself. There is a passion for drama present in all the publications and a firm conviction of its educational and personal value. However, without tackling the key question of how to get rid of ideological glasses, then, following Bond, we remain vision-impaired in our attempts to understand our world and ourselves in it.

An immediate indication of the continuing influence of Brecht is to be found in the number of references to him, as opposed to Bond, in the indexes of these publications: 69 to 18 in favour of Brecht and many of them over several pages. To find that there were only 18 index references to Edward Bond in some thirty comparatively recent drama books is a bit of an eye opener. Take Schonmann's *Key Concepts in Theatre/Drama Education* (2011), for example, where in some 55 papers by leading drama educators from around the world there are 11 index references to Brecht, some multi-page, and none for Bond. He is regarded by many as the leading contemporary UK playwright who has spent the last 18 years or so writing plays for Big Brum Theatre in Education Company. I have been present at the world premiere of his plays in a Birmingham primary school. He has also been writing plays for worldwide audiences yet the relevance of his work seems comparatively unrecognized by most of these writers working with young people.

As well as ignoring the problem of ideology, most of these publications set aside any examination of the growing social and cultural crisis that is the context of the drama methods being promoted. Many limit their role to serving the curriculum, for example Kempe and Nicholson (2007), Dickenson and Neelands (2006), and Winston and Tandy (2001). It is as though drama teachers feel they have to steer clear of politics rather than see drama in this period as essentially political. Where there is a lack of fear about being political, as in Lewis and Rainer (2012), who offer a useful analysis of the reactionary approach to the curriculum in the UK and who also have useful process dramas dealing with political/social topics, for example around the life and death of Sophie Scholl and dealing with conflict in Northern Ireland, there is still no real examination of what sort of drama is needed to deal with our ideologically distorted vision. There is also evidence in many publications of the widespread use of Neelands's conventions. Farmer (2011), for example, bases his book almost entirely around the use of conventions. This use of conventions invariably leads to a distanced reflective mode rather than the direct engagement producing the *metaxis* effect advocated by Bolton.

Originally my intention was to report briefly on each of the books, but unsatisfied with such a cursory treatment of them, I began to extend my survey. This, however, proved to be too much of a distraction from my main pursuit: exploring the problem of developing a relevant form of post-Brechtian drama other than those described in Lehmann, Nicholson, and Carroll *et al.* and, in the end, finding a way of giving due respect to every book defeated me. However, I do feel it important to substantiate my claim that in some instances we are travelling backwards instead of forwards. There were some areas in some of the books that I found disturbing.

One of the most disappointing was West's *Inspired Drama Teaching: A practical guide for teachers* (2011). I found myself reading guidance that seemed to come from Brian Way (concentration exercises), and Peter Slade-type work (running round saying 'hello') and, in a chapter on the elements of drama, this advice to develop characterization:

> **Gestures** – I could fold my arms and glare at the men. This would show I was disgusted with them.
> **Voice** – I could snarl and bark out my orders. This would show I was in authority.
> **Movement** – I could turn my back on the others. This would show that I was in control.
>
> (West, 2011: 60)

This was followed by practice in showing the emotions of the character:

- In pairs, look as surprised as you possibly can. Imagine someone has told you that you have won first prize in a competition. When surprised, your eyes may become wider and the whites of your eyes should become more pronounced. Perhaps your eyebrows might become curved and raised.
- In pairs, look as frightened as you possibly can. Imagine you have seen a ghost and the ghost is floating towards you. Again you need to concentrate on facial expression. A frightened person might not look directly into another's eyes. Wrinkles may appear on their forehead.
- In pairs, and concentrating on your facial expression, display anger. An angry person's eyebrows will narrow and his/her eyes might appear to be 'popping out of their sockets'. Maybe their nostrils will flare ...

> (West, 2011: 60)

Gavin Bolton criticized this sort of drama teaching thirty years ago (Bolton, 1984). He was describing a research project in the USA that was undertaken in 1972 and commenting on lessons where the teacher asked the children to be:

> sad, happy and surprised in turn. The sad girl rubbed her eyes, commenting 'Oh, I'm so sad'; the happy boy exuberantly jumped up and down and commented 'Oh, I'm so happy. The sun is out.' Later, anger and fright entered the parade.
>
> (Bolton, 1984: 102)

Bolton strongly opposes the idea of switching on and portraying an emotion: '"Characterisation packages" are in my view a total irrelevance to drama and to education', the participants should concentrate 'not on whether he or she is signalling an emotion but with getting on with solving whatever problem is to hand' (Bolton, 1984: 102).

Unfortunately this approach appears again in Tandy and Howell (2010):

> The teacher then calls out a word or phrase that describes an emotion, e.g. anger, distress, fear, loneliness, confusion, at which point the partners will stop and hold each other's gaze in the manner of the word. The teacher then says, 'Go' and they walk on again, until the next word is called.
>
> (Tandy and Howell, 2010: 3)

Another example of what I consider unfortunate is to be found in Cuthbertson (2011). Her example, a school production of *Romeo and Juliet* that has 'as its main theme a strong anti-knife, anti-gang message' (83), seems to me a total travesty. The work seems to have had a history of great success and, I feel sure, was greatly enjoyed by the participants and by the parents and audience but it seems to me to go along with the sensationalism and populism that pervade the theatre in the UK today. This is captured in Edward Bond's words quoted earlier: 'English theatre [is] in a state of decline ... "Don't look for a meaning. Watch the spectacle"' (Bond, 2012a).

In Shakespeare's play, Romeo and Juliet are growing up in a dysfunctional adult world where the *adults* are the vandals who start the feuds (wars) that young people get caught up in. It is a world of arranged marriages rather than of true love. Romeo is not even present at the first fight caused by the servants aping their masters – he has been out all night dreaming of his latest love, Rosaline. The law (like today's magistrates who send the young to prison) condemns Romeo to exile, directly leading to his and Juliet's deaths, thus creating a tragedy rather than solving a problem.

Two adults, the Nurse and the Friar, claim to have the best interests of the young at heart and help them marry secretly, yet both betray that trust at the last moment. The Nurse urges Juliet to marry Paris, her father's choice, 'Romeo's a dish cloth compared to him' and, later, the Friar's 'I dare no longer stay' signals that he is leaving Juliet to her fate so as to save his own neck. Shakespeare's provocation is that there are no adults entirely on the side of young people. The kindest, most student-centred teacher will betray you to authority in the end! And in the final moments of the play is the hint that nothing will change as Montague and Capulet begin to brag about who will build the richest memorial to the two young people.

Yet in Cuthbertson's production, the focus is not on the adult perpetrators of the tragedy but on gang fights between hoodies who circle each other on BMX bikes. In what seems the ultimate example of creating sensational effects rather than drama, Juliet has a hallucinogenic nightmare when she takes the drug the Friar has given her:

> So we create a scene showing that nightmare – a crazy hen-night party, a dead Tybalt walking through, Paris as a stripper, Romeo trying to reach her but unable to. This short scene is generally considered one of the highlights of the whole production. If extra scenes illuminate something, adding an extra dimension without distorting the play, put them in!
>
> (Cuthberton, 2011: 90)

So drawing a moustache onto the *Mona Lisa* could be a useful addition to Leonardo da Vinci's art. I rest my case!

This was not the only area that disturbed me during my research. I was disappointed to find authors still recommending acting out a story, for example Winston and Tandy (2001: 22), Woolland (2010: 111), and Farmer (2011). You cannot act out a story. It needs to be transformed into another art form where there is time to open up an event to explore what lies between the people in that situation. Again, drama is often conflated with other art forms such as film and television in, for example, Nicholson (2000: 7), Winston and Tandy (2001: vi), Carroll *et al.* (2006: 11) and Woolland (2010: 1). Drama is a unique art form where the events are not presented to us through the eye of the camera/director. It is the live presence offered by live drama that enables the participant/audience to deal with unmediated reality.

Drama still being seen as communication was another disturbing area, for example in West (2011: 5) and Nicholson (2000: 2). Drama is not a form of communication. What is communicated in *Hamlet*? Rather Shakespeare asks us a lot of unanswered questions. There is also evidence that knowledge and the curriculum are still being *delivered*, in, for example, Toye and Prendiville (2000: 7) and Woolland (2010: 133). You cannot deliver knowledge. It has to be discovered through active learning and made your own.

Drama is described as a symbolization process in many publications, for example in Bowell and Heap (2001: 9) and Woolland (2010: 5). This seems to me to gloss over the whole problem of what symbols are; this requires an understanding of the contribution made by poststructuralist theory and semiotics. Bond, for example, never uses symbols in drama and would deny it should be a symbolizing process. This will be taken up more fully later. And finally, because there is no room for more, drama is still seen as pretending, for example in Woolland (2010: 2) and Winston and Tandy (2001: viii). Drama is being, not pretending.

I started this section with the aim of checking if there had been major innovations in form that took us in a useful direction to meet the challenges of the present period; to determine to what extent Bond's influence might have begun to replace Brechtian (and Stanislavskian) influences in drama teaching; to see if I could find support for my belief that a conventions approach is widespread; and to examine how ideology is being tackled.

It is clear that the problem of ideology is not being explored at all in any significant way in classroom drama, apart from those beginning attempts to take into account the theory behind Bondian theatre. Distancing (Brechtian) influences are still widespread through the use of conventions, and Stanislavskian naturalism is still present, for example in the work on characterization above. The only conscious developments of form seem to be those from post-Brechtian performance theory and those placing drama in the digital age and mixing media together.

In Part Two I set out my own approach to some areas of classroom drama practice.

Notes

[1] This has just been made even more difficult. Michael Gove, UK Secretary of State for Education has, in March 2013, removed Drama as a named subject from the revised draft National Curriculum Key Stages 1 to 3 (that is, up to the age of 14). Interestingly Richard Courtney, a well-known early writer on drama in education, claimed 'to have evidence that right-wing Prime Minister Margaret Thatcher herself gave the orders for drama to be dropped from the new National Curriculum' (O'Toole and Stinson, 2009: 197). Is there something inherently worrying about drama in the curriculum for Conservative leading figures?

[2] My thanks to Mike Fleming for finding this quotation for me. I searched high and low but still missed it. Mike found it in a few hours.

[3] Heathcote had used this label to describe her drama in the famous film of her work

Three Looms Waiting, (1972) namely 'Drama is just a man in a mess.'

[4] I remember clearly the moment when we realized this. Gavin Bolton and I were preparing to teach a workshop together in Canada in the mid-1970s (really this meant assisting him teach the workshop he had planned and me trying to keep up with his thinking). He had been to a lecture given by Heathcote and as we started planning (I scribbling away on sheet after sheet of paper, he sitting still with his eyes closed until he had finished planning it) he turned to me and said 'It's not about "gut-level drama" after all. It's about distancing.'

[5] It may be worth noting that Bolton's comments written above were all approved by Heathcote, who read a draft of the chapter.

[6] I have discussed this fully in Davis (2009) and aim to do no more here than provide a basic perspective.

[7] The article was written for the SCYPT Journal, *The Standing Conference of Young People's Theatre*, not *The Standing Council for Young People's Theatre* as Neelands has it in O'Connor (2010: xvii). I write this not out of pedantry but out of respect for that extraordinary organization, which led an international movement for TIE. It is deserving of respect rather than the continuing witch-hunt type phraseology of calling it 'Trotskyist inspired'. There are now, and were then, many Marxist political parties and groups owing their allegiance to Trotsky rather than Stalin and, certainly, those parties and groups did *not* come together to form SCYPT. It was founded to further the artistic aims of theatre for young people.

[8] This is dealt with directly in Katafiasz (2005) and Davis (2009).

[9] The 'representational', that is the 'living through' mode, is acknowledged as a very minor part of the conventions approach.

[10] Anderson, M. (2012); Blatner, A. (ed.) with Wiener, D.J. (2007); Bowell, P. and Heap, B.S. (2001); Braverman, D. (2002); Carroll, J., Anderson, M. and Cameron, D. (2006); Coventon, J. (ed.) (2011); Dickenson, R. and Neelands, J. (2006); Doona, J. (2013a); Doona, J. (2013b); Farmer, D. (2011); Fleming, M. (2011); Kempe, A. and Nicholson, H. (2007); Lewis, M. and Rainer, J. (2012); Nicholson, H. (ed.) (2000); Nicholson, H. (2005); Nicholson, H. (2009); Nicholson, H. (2011); O'Connor, P. (2010); O'Regan, T. (2004); O'Toole, J., Stinson, M. and Moore, T. (2009); Prendergast, M. and Saxton, J. (eds) (2009); Schonmann, S. (ed.) (2011); Tandy, M. and Howell, J. (2010); Taylor, P. and Warner, D. (eds) (2006); Toye, N. and Prendiville, F. (2000); West, K. (2011); Wheeller, M. (2010); Winston, J. and Tandy, M. (2001); Woolland, B. (2008); Woolland, B. (2010); Wooster, R. (2007).

Part Two

2

Chapter 3

Key dimensions of classroom drama

Introduction

Classroom drama is a strange phrase, used in the past by Gavin Bolton. It usefully identifies all sorts of drama in education: in the classroom, drama studio or school hall, as opposed to theatre for performance. I am particularly interested in what has come to be called process drama – another potentially misleading name, as process is also a product and the participant is also, importantly, a percipient, most importantly from inside the role. Heathcote described this process as 'self-spectating', but this does not quite complete the picture. A slight gap is implied, which could allow the process of introspection to be in two stages. I do something and I am monitoring what I do. I prefer the notion of *metaxis*, with the implication of being in two states at the same time, which enables the two states to be fought out internally. In role I stole some money, which I would not do in real life – or would I? Why did I take that action in role? There needs to be an impulse to critical self-reflection from within that process. It is the self-spectating from within the dual role, *metaxis*, which perhaps more closely captures the mode of involvement I am seeking and it needs to be provoked by an impulse provided by the drama event in which the role finds itself. It may be useful to clarify the meaning of *metaxis* as it is pivotal to what follows.

Metaxis enters drama in education from Boal via various sources, for example Bolton (1992) and O'Toole (1992). The word comes from the Greek *metaxu* meaning 'between' and 'in' and is the place of spirits according to Plato, between humans and gods, belonging to both and making the universe an interconnected whole (Linds, 2005). However, by the time the term came to be used in drama education it is used in a vital different way to how it is used in Boal. In Boal, *metaxis* is 'the state of belonging completely and simultaneously to two different, *autonomous* worlds ... The oppressed must *forget the real world* which was the origin of the image and play with the image itself in its artistic embodiment' (Boal, 1995: 43–4, emphasis added). In Bolton the meaning is quite different, 'the power ... of the experience stem[s] from fully recognising that one is in two social contexts *at the same time*

(Bolton, 1992: 11, emphasis added). It is this power of 'being' in two worlds at the same time that underlies the sort of drama I go on to describe, and I shall be using *metaxis* in the way Bolton describes it rather than the way Boal defines it. I think this is what Bolton means when he writes about 'making' drama in order to 'be' in role and I aim to use 'being' in role in the same way. In what follows I use 'making' drama as the whole process of building an engagement with a drama event where 'being' in role and 'living through' become the central aims, with *metaxis* as the key component.

I regard Bolton's *Acting in Classroom Drama* (1998) as the most important book written about process drama. The focus of the book, and his PhD from which the book is taken, is on one sentence of David Hornbrook's with which he profoundly disagrees: 'It is my contention that conceptually there is nothing which differentiates the child acting in the classroom from the actor on the stage of the theatre' (Hornbook, 1989: 104). Two hundred and seventy-three pages later, after surveying a hundred years of drama in education history, he comes to the conclusion that it is necessary to insist on 'seeing "making" as a special category of acting behaviour, especially when a "living through", that is, a "teacher-in-role-led" approach to drama is adopted' (Bolton, 1998: 273–4; Bolton, 2010c: 40). He separates out 'making' drama as a unique form of acting behaviour. I concur with this, except that I think it is possible for children to 'make' drama, with the 'living through' dimension, on their own without teacher in role guiding the process.

Bolton's other forms of acting behaviour he lists as 'presenting' and 'performing'. I tend to use 'making' to describe the tripartite process of working for those moments of 'living through' that form the key moments of the experience: I am making it happen (the role building in the drama event); it is happening to me (the living through experience); I am conscious of it happening to me (producing the *metaxis* effect). I have also included 'presenting' in some of the examples below, as I think on occasions the presenting work can shade into living through. More on this later.

Bolton draws attention to 'making' as a 'hugely important educational and dramatic tool' and he warns that 'To ignore "living through" drama, as some recent publications appear to do, is to deprive our pupils of a firm basis for understanding dramatic art' (Bolton, 2010c: 43). Neelands is one of those he is referring to who misdescribes this sort of drama by writing about it as follows:

> Drama in Education ... holds to the idea that by 'living through' human experiences in a 'realistic' and 'life-like' way in real time young people will discover the 'truth' of human existence which

they can only imagine and never really know. Living through the experiences of peoples who are temporally, spatially, culturally, and socio-economically different 'as if' these experience[s] were actually happening here and now for the participants in a process drama is seen as being more truthful and 'life-like' a learning experience than other more stylised and self-reflexive forms of theatre.

(Neelands, 2006: 146)

This would be true without the worked for engagement that leads to the participants being in two worlds at the same time: the *metaxis* effect. It is why it is necessary to build this into the structure, which process Neelands mocks as the 'four hours or more ... "building investment" and "belief"' (Neelands, 2006: 146). He comes closer to the way I see drama working when he writes 'we can only ever learn more about our own personal and collective self through imagining ourselves differently' (146). However, I would not see it as imagining ourselves differently, which implies the outside looking in, but drama provoking a situation where we have the chance to *create* our human self and become different. Of course, we may not take the opportunity and the drama experience may simply reinforce the *status quo*.

In Part Two, I outline the basics of my own approach to 'making' drama and try to provide enough examples and argument to claim it makes some sort of coherent theory. By process drama I mean drama that takes the subject matter explored in world drama, uses key components of theatre as an art form, and involves a teacher working with a class of young people to 'make' drama together. Drama is the art form that puts under a spotlight key moments that expose the social pressures that enter us, and which we burden ourselves with and place on each other as we share this planet together, and raises key questions for us to examine and consider. To do so means creating events that bring us into that spotlight together, rather than being outside looking on. It is drama not in preparation for performance but entailing building an engagement with role through improvisations that may be presented to each other but which centrally will involve a 'being' in role event or events, in immediate time and space. Although there is no audience outside the participants, even and especially when 'being' in role, key dimensions of percipience are present: a key dimension of interacting with others in a dialogic sense, which is more than inter-acting; and a key dimension of introspecting that is more than just self-spectating. By dialogic I mean, following Bakhtin (see Morris, 1994), the interpenetration of consciousnesses that takes place in dialogic intercourse. As Bakhtin puts it, commenting on Dostoevsky's writing:

> In Dostoevsky, consciousness never gravitates toward itself but is always found in intense relationship with another consciousness. Every experience, every thought of a character is internally dialogic, adorned with polemic, filled with struggle ...
>
> (Bakhtin cited in Morris, 1994: 14)

Pretty well all that follows is not original – far from it. It is learnt mainly from Gavin Bolton, Dorothy Heathcote, Cecily O'Neill and Geoff Gillham. Perhaps the only area that might have a claim to originality is in devising a way that young people can create a 'living through' experience without the structuring presence of the teacher in role (TiR). Bolton tends to see TiR as a necessary precondition of this sort of involvement, which he refers to as '"living through's" dependence on "teacher-in-role"' (Bolton, 2010c: 39). I suggest that there are forms where this 'living through' is possible without TiR and I set out below the necessary preconditions for this to be possible.

I have tried to make the following accounts of drama theory and practice useful for the starting drama teacher. I ask the indulgence of experienced drama teachers if I am stating what is obvious for them. I also seek the indulgence of those who might wonder why I am repeating well-known theory. My defence is that I suspect a lot of this theory is no longer readily available to new teachers who want to use drama and I also need to set it out in order to explore what aspects of it might be developed.

Mantle of the Expert and process drama as art

It is useful to distinguish between process drama as art and Mantle of the Expert. In a recent article Luke Abbott (2011), the leading figure in Mantle of the Expert.com, which has patented the term,[1] set out his own definitions of the two. While I have the greatest respect for Luke Abbott and his work I find it difficult to go along with his view of the relationship between the two areas.

He argues that the informed drama teacher is likely to have three strands at her disposal: inquiry and investigation methods; drama for learning (DFL); and Mantle of the Expert (MoE) or a combination of DFL and MoE. I have no disagreement with the way he describes MoE – as an expert in the field he knows the area far better than I do. He defines it as:

> Mantle of the Expert ... uses whole group viewpoints, by creating a responsible team and imagined 'client' through tasks. Learners then decide to take a series of thought through actions to move forwards to tackling their client's commission. As in other

> dramatic [*sic*] methods, the class represents their engagements by
> using symbolic, expressive and iconic behaviours.
>
> (Abbott, 2011: 23)

I am taking it as read that the responsible team is in role and that 'team' is deliberately general to cover the notion of an enterprise as well as more general but coherent groups of people. I am also reading the last three forms of representation, 'symbolic, expressive and iconic', as referring to Bruner's modes of representation: 'enactive, iconic, symbolic' (Bruner, 1974: 316).

However, the way Abbott defines process drama and the way he relates it to MoE approaches is worth exploring.

I am uncomfortable with the term 'drama for learning' as a way of describing the sort of process drama I intend to depict. It carries the strong sense of there needing to be a learning outcome. Hiding behind this could be the implication of the need to teach something other than drama form, and behind that the value system of the teacher and a moral or curriculum imperative. Abbott does not intend this, and sets out a definition of process drama as coming from the 'North East School of Drama in Education' (Abbott, 2011: 22), presumably speaking for teachers influenced by Heathcote and Bolton. It is a definition that avoids the danger I indicate above, but the term itself could lead in this direction. He defines Drama for Learning as:

> Consciously [using] the fictive expressive imagination to explore
> moments of living life that are designed for exploration and
> indeed have unanswered questions in the chosen contexts as well
> as exploring and reflecting on how people behave, think and do.
>
> (Abbott, 2011: 22)

As before, I am taking it as read that the fictive expression is in role rather than, say, in writing. And I am understanding the difference between behaving and doing as the former being reactive and the latter proactive. The term 'expressive imagination', however, I feel needs further explanation. To me it implies bringing an imagination to bear that already takes a certain point of view. That may mean that the drama situation is set up to confound and disrupt that view. This would be heading in a more useful direction for me, but neither the use nor the term is elaborated further. The moments of 'living life' I take to mean 'living through' moments. And having unanswered questions is useful, although I feel that 'exploring and reflecting on how people behave, think and do' carries too much of the reflective. My preference is for the immediate in-role engagement with a drama event which insists that the imagination has to re-work what is being experienced into new ways of seeing and understanding the world and our relationship to it. These unclear areas apart, the examples of DFL and MoE that Abbott then sets out usefully allow us to compare and contrast these two modes of using drama.

As an example of DFL, he suggests a giant who has fallen down the stairs in a large castle and is lying very still. He can be seen through the letter box but for some reason the door cannot be opened. His mother is very worried. Can these young people help (4- and 5-year-olds) as they can get through the letter box? But how can they make sure they are safe? Would it be better to wait? This seems an example of the expressive imagination at work: we bring our existing knowledge to work on a new situation. This is different to having your present knowledge of the world challenged by the event encountered.

For the MoE method the teacher would establish a responsible team of 'giant-nurses' to act on behalf of the client, the mother. Abbott lists several questions that presumably belong to the MoE approach but actually seem more to belong to the DFL example or, presumably, could belong to either method or are just the 'inquiry and investigative methods' illustrated. Abbott suggests, for example: Suppose the giant is dead? Suppose the giant thinks it is our fault? Suppose the giant is in need of treatment? This is where the example becomes less clear.

However, I think there is enough here to enable me to clarify how I see the difference between MoE and process drama. If we can ease the participants away from being 4 to 5 years old and make them 9 to 10 years, it might be possible to use the same event to bring the discussion into a wider arena. I hope this is not too manipulative. Later, I will attempt to use the same arguments and illustrate them for the younger age group.

At the moment in both examples the given circumstances are not to be questioned. This is part of what happens in the world and we need to respond. What I find missing is the social context of the event. At the moment it is asocial, but what is surrounding it? Has he been experimenting with alcohol? Has he locked himself in to have a taste of his father's drink in secret? Has he been drinking and being drunk has fallen down the stairs? Why would he want to try a drink? What is it in the giant world that has led him to want to try alcohol? Or, has he been violent towards his mother and she has locked him in but is too ashamed to admit it? Or again, what are the children doing in someone else's world? What do they know about giant culture? What right have they to intrude to 'help' in this foreign land? Are they being manipulated because they do not understand the culture? We could go on inventing more questions until we found one that fitted the situation and that group of students. These all imply a social context and enable us to examine the personal in the social and the social in the personal. As it stands the social context is not up for consideration. We accept the world we find ourselves in and try to do the best we can within it.

If we were to leave them as 4- to 5-year-olds we might focus more on helping as best we can in the short term and leave it at that or try to help figure out what has gone wrong. Why was the young giant left alone in the house? Where has his mother been? Perhaps out to work and she has to leave her son in the house alone and locked in. Is this a good thing to do? Is there any way round it, especially as she now seems to have lost the key? And so on.

I see this lack of questioning the values in the social context as the inherent weakness in the MoE method. It is too often caught within the present parameters of society and within those parameters we work to develop a positive human ethos and try to move things forward as best we can. All well and good you may say. However, the key question is: how can young people come to a more realistic view of the nature of society and how they are manipulated into being by it? And how can they continually renew their relationship to it and their own value system? In other words: how can the drama provoke a situation where they have the opportunity to create their humanity? Or not, as the case may be. This is my hesitation about calling it drama for learning. There is too often an urge for the teacher to pursue his own (necessarily limited) view of the world.

This argument is more clearly demonstrated in the MoE example that precedes the giant drama in the same article. The students are young Palestinians who, in role, have the responsibility to protect a 1,000-year-old olive tree that is under threat. A contractor is going to build a store for medical supplies and he is to build a road that will come near to the farmland and the tree. Who will care for the tree when it is threatened? Then comes the get-out clause that takes it out of its actual social context or any social context.

> In the first instance we are avoiding any reference to military matters such as borders, war, etc. as these contexts carry too much power to control and are 'non-negotiable forces'. For me [Abbott] anyway, our young learners will need to take ownership through 'tensions' established by the power TO INFLUENCE rather than 'conflicts' associated with power to resist subjugation, or to physically fight and so on – though I repeat – this is in the FIRST INSTANCE!
>
> (Abbott, 2011: 18, capitals in original)

The problem is we never come to the second instance. It seems to me just not feasible to decontextualize it, especially in a country occupied for 56 years where permission to build a store, let alone a road, would be very difficult to obtain. Here is a partial glimpse of the real context:

> Israeli policies and practices in the West Bank and Gaza have included extensive use of collective punishments such as curfews, house demolitions and closure of roads, schools and community institutions. Hundreds of Palestinian political activists have been deported to Jordan or Lebanon, tens of thousands of acres of Palestinian land have been confiscated, and thousands of trees have been uprooted. Since 1967, over 300,000 Palestinians have been imprisoned without trial, and over half a million have been tried in the Israeli military court system. Torture of Palestinian prisoners has been a common practice since at least 1971, and dozens of people have died in detention from abuse or neglect. Israeli officials have claimed that harsh measures and high rates of imprisonment are necessary to thwart terrorism. According to Israel, Palestinian terrorism includes all forms of opposition to the occupation (including non-violence).
>
> (MERIP, 2013)

Abbott adds 'In the education of the human curriculum we hear in any case how the tensions of war can be alleviated through humane actions that are healing. Medical teams allowed through checkpoints for example' (Abbott, 2011: 18). Humane actions are all well and good but what about the Palestinians desperately needing to get to medical help turned away at the checkpoints; women giving birth at the checkpoint because they have not been allowed through? Abbott's example is not part of a human curriculum but of a humane curriculum, which is an entirely different thing. A humane curriculum I see as one stemming from a particular type of liberal ideological agenda promoting kindness and tolerance towards people and animals. This leaves out the when and when not to adapt advocated by Bolton. A human curriculum I see as one where the students are enabled to ask questions, to find answers, and to express their intuitions and understandings about themselves and everything about them without being led by any ideological stance. There is a real danger here that in MoE work the students are encouraged to make the best of a bad world rather than come to a clearer understanding of the real nature of that world and how it shapes and influences each one of us.

However, MoE also has positive qualities. It reverses the usual teacher–student relationship and removes the fear of failure. The students and the teacher pursue knowledge together in an active learning approach. Within the framework of having to teach a reactionary curriculum it is an entirely progressive approach that empowers the child, encourages active learning, and takes the child into much wider areas than the narrow enclaves of a traditional national curriculum. This makes MoE one of the most forward-looking teaching/learning methods available with a school curriculum framework. For this reason I have always taught it but must confess that I have tweaked it to bring in those social context dimensions I am claiming are missing in the above example. My key point is that MoE is not using drama as art: that is to create events that cause instability and force the individual to reorientate him or herself in the world. MoE uses drama to work from within the system to try to move things on as far as possible. I cannot stop myself needing to work to undermine the system itself.

After this attempt to clarify the relationship between process drama and MoE approaches I return to what I see as basic areas of knowledge for the teacher who aims to make process drama with her students. In some cases I have set out these theory areas as workshop exercises for student teachers, both because this might be a useful way to visualize the areas and also because it is the way I have taught them and tried them out. I have most usually worked with teachers wanting to develop the knowledge and skills employed by drama teachers, or with people experienced in drama but not experienced in drama in education. It might also be possible for drama teachers to adapt these exercises for their own students.

Notes

[1] Too many people were setting up companies claiming to train teachers in MoE, in some cases over a weekend and charging a lot of money for it; the training being quite insufficient to carry this sort of work forward. Heathcote suggested they patent the term. For more information on this and the history of MoE see Abbott, 2013. For some people this patenting has been a step too far.

Chapter 4

Towards a theory of 'making' drama

A basic theory of 'making' drama would need to include: the nature of the art form and the components involved in structuring improvised drama; the making of meaning and layers of meaning; framing the participants; the modes of involvement available in process drama; the sequencing and internal coherence of the structure; protection into role; secondary symbolism and the angle of connection; play for class and play for teacher; and student role-playing. While there is not space to discuss them here, ideally I would include sections on teacher in role, the nature of emotion in drama, and a large section on semiotics. To cover all key areas I would have needed a whole book – as did O'Toole in *The Process of Drama: Negotiating art and meaning* (O'Toole, 1992), a much underrated book in my opinion. I will, however, cover the uses of imagination and reason, and drama, society and ideology in Part Three, along with something on semiotics.

It is usual to suggest that in process drama the teacher and the students necessarily share the roles of playwright, director, actors and audience. I have indicated below which areas I see belonging to whom: those that are the joint responsibility of students and teacher; those that are solely the responsibility of the student; and those over which the teacher has complete control or at least the sole responsibility to initiate (see the text box at the end of this section). My aim is to set out the essentials of a theory of making drama with examples of related practice. The drama teacher, having worked out a theory of his or her own will be able to work out an infinite number of structures and drama events.

I start with the nature of the art form; the aspects of the art form key to making drama.

The nature of the art form

I am proposing that knowledge of how the art form works is an area of joint knowledge and responsibility. For students new to drama the responsibility devolves almost entirely onto the teacher but the experience of making drama begins the process of induction into the knowledge that the teacher is using so that over a period of time, probably years in a school curriculum, the students develop an ability to understand how the art form is working and an ability to take their share of the responsibility for forming it. It is the third of Bolton's aims quoted earlier: 'To help the student gain understanding of and satisfaction from the medium of drama' (Bolton, 1976: 1).

To begin at the beginning, I invite a student who has laces in her shoes or trainers to come into the centre of the circle of students and ask her to unlace her trainer and then tie it up. She does so. This is a *real life* action outside the art form.[1]

Then I ask her to unlace it again and imagine she is a young child just at the age of wanting to tie her own shoelaces unaided. She is told that no matter how hard she tries, she cannot manage to do so. We watch her try. She tries and tries again but somehow the lace always manages to refuse to do what she wants it to and what it does when her mother ties it for her. This is *simulation*. It is a step towards drama as an art form. The student has taken on a role but it remains in a one-to-one simulation of the actual event.

I invite another student to join her in the circle and ask the new student to take on the role of the child's mother. I ask them to imagine it is a Sunday and the local supermarket will close at 4 p.m. It is 3.15 and it will take a quarter of an hour to walk to the supermarket. It is the time she needs to go as all the last minute near out-of-date bargains will be on sale: meat maybe, fish maybe, and other key items she cannot normally afford. She is a single parent struggling to make ends meet. If she leaves it too late most or all of the bargains will be gone. She has to take her child with her. The given is that she has a close and loving relationship with her child and believes children should grow up to be as independent as possible. Time is running out and the child is given the objective that she will not go before she has tied her shoes completely unaided. When I have tried this with students the child is usually sitting on the floor of a poorly furnished kitchen, absorbed in the task, and the mother is standing to the side looking on. The mother usually runs through the whole gamut of tactics: waiting patiently; then bending down to offer advice; then praising every time the child nearly succeeds; then crouching down trying to help with the child swivelling round to face in the opposite direction; bribing the child with the promise of sweets if she lets mother tie the lace; and finally threatening punishment and forcibly taking over. In the background I have been reminding the mother of the time countdown. This is now *moving towards* the art form. Meaning-making has become the central aim of the activity.

It has been the same action in all three situations but this last action has taken on different meanings as the circumstances have changed. The final scene could be part of a drama structure or a play about education. Through the dramatic actions of the parent she recapitulates the major theories of learning and the corresponding theories of teaching: from active discovery learning; to structured interventions; the offering of rewards (stars) for good work; to behaviourist shaping; to punishment of failure. There has been productive distortion of the action to promote the possibility of exploring meaning. Components of the art form have been inserted and these can be analysed as follows.

Components of the art form

Roles: the students have each taken on a role that they have been able to slip into easily. The closer to the real-life experience of the students the less protection into role is necessary; less being the operative word rather than none at all. Here there has been time to get used to the situation, starting in silence and moving towards minimal dialogue and then mainly from the mother. These roles do not involve a complex process of character building. The use of the term role implies the student is trying to capture the essential features of either a mother or a young child. They will be drawing on their own experiences and that of observed others. This is part of the *metaxis* process. This does not mean they will be cardboard cut-outs. They need to be real people but without the lengthy preparation of a Stanislavskian approach. They will be drawing on their own knowledge of the role and on themselves so they can form a believable relationship with the other roles in the drama. In particular they will adopt a particular attitude in any scene.

Attitudes: To begin to relate to another role it is useful to give or find an attitude. Here the given for the mother is that she has a loving, caring attitude to her daughter and believes in fostering her independence. This gives her an attitude that will affect how she strives to achieve her objective. The child is likely to accept this but, if she plays her objective for all she is worth (a necessary skill students need to learn), she will be focusing on her task and her own immediate needs. Her own attitude is likely to flow from her mother's: accepting and maintaining the good relationship but concentrating on something else.

Objectives and counter-objectives: The mother and the child have each been given an objective: the mother, to get to the supermarket in time to get bargains; the child, to tie her own shoelace unaided. These are straight Stanislavskian objectives, the 'I want ...' that I find useful. It is probably the only dimension I keep from Stanislavski. The fact that they are counter-objectives gives rise to the imperative tension of the scene.

Tension: All drama explores the headaches the social world gives us and which we pass on to each other as we share the planet together. It is the art form *par excellence* that examines these situations and tension is the key descriptor. Without tension in the event there is no drama. However, it is *not* conflict. The moment conflict appears that is the end of the dramatic episode. Tension is immanence of conflict. All through *Hamlet* the tension of the desire for revenge predominates. It seems as though it will be put to rest when Hamlet thinks it is his uncle behind the arras and aims to kill him, only to find it is old Polonius. If it had been his uncle, it could have been the end of the play. As it is the conflict only comes, not as an act of revenge for his father's murder, but because his mother has been poisoned. Then the medieval takes over from the Renaissance man and blood is spilled everywhere. The tension of an improvised scene is usefully held in place by a constraint.

Constraint: In our scene of the mother and child she is constrained from tying the shoelace for the child because she believes in fostering her child's independence. This acts as a brake on her impatience and need to leave for the shop. It is most often what is missing in a classroom improvisation when one of the pair holds up his hand to say 'We've finished', after about one minute of role-play. It is the way time is slowed down in drama.

Time: One of the problems in drama is how to slow down time without it appearing to be slowed down. Allowed to improvise a drama about a robbery, young children will just zoom around the drama studio in a police car, jump out after the third trip round the studio and chase the robber around another three times until they jump on him or her and put their hands up to say they have finished. All the time the key question is how to structure the situation so there is time to explore what lies between these people in that situation. For example, what sort of interaction takes place when the police officer catches the robber to find it is his or her child? Constraint is a key component of a drama event to slow the action down. This is what Heathcote would call 'volume' development of the story.

Storyline and plot: There is a minimal storyline here but it is still present. Will the mother get to the shop on time? In our little story the mother is a single parent and has to make every penny count. The storyline structures what happens next and the plot structures the subtext or the content of the play. The story develops as the mother tries different tactics: to help, to bribe, to threaten. The plot thickens as the child resists each offer of help or bribe or threat. The interaction of these two structures the meaning of the drama, as elaborated below, and gives rise to the text of the drama.

Pre-text and context: Cecily O'Neill (1995) usefully introduces the notion of pre-text, pointing out that every play starts in the middle. There are key events that have taken place before the play starts. Hamlet's uncle has murdered his father and married his mother. The Capulets and Montagues have been feuding for years. These are pre-texts. In the kitchen drama the pre-text is the given of the hard-up single parent and the need to get to the supermarket. The drama also has a context, a location or, as Bond calls it, the site of the drama. This is the most suitable place for the interactions to take place that will add significance to the content. In our little drama it is in a poorly furnished kitchen. The above all help to feed into the event or dramatic action.

Dramatic action: The event is most usefully held in a dramatic action rather than just an ocean of words, which is what classroom drama often becomes. The action focuses the meaning. What is the action through which the meaning of the event can be explored? In our example it is the tying of the shoelace. In the opening of *King Lear* it is the sharing of Lear's kingdom. In one production of the play the map of England took up the whole of the stage and Lear walked about it, parcelling it up, clearly demonstrating he owned the land. In *Romeo and Juliet* it is the opening quarrel and fight between the servants that goes straight to the heart of the play. It is not just a discussion between people. Dramatic action is key to the structuring of the drama. The danger of improvisation is that it conjures up a sea of words with the students only in role through what they are saying. A key part of the dramatic action's meanings are held in the **body language, objects, and the images** created. These are essential ingredients to make a drama event. (More on meanings and layers of meanings below.)

Drama event: The event is the drama situation that enables layers of meaning to be explored. (Bond also uses the term 'drama event' but it has a different meaning to that being developed here.) It needs to have important implications for the participants. If the mother is finally faced with either dragging the child out or going hungry in the following week and having the young child shout out how false she has been in encouraging independence (not in those words) the whole scene is nearer to what I would call a drama event. A scene that builds the drama structure may involve simple situation exercises such as this one or more complicated, longer process dramas, one of which is exemplified later.

The above can be condensed as shown in Figure 4.1.

Key components of a drama event in process drama
An **event** with strong implications for the participants and heightened **tension** in a **context** which has a **pre-text** with **roles** (not characters) embodying an **attitude** to an other or others – pursuing **counter-objectives** – slowing down **time** – under the pressure of **constraints** – the **event** revealing and **focusing layers of meaning (sub-text)** through **dramatic action, objects, images, body language and words**, especially the **language register** (immediately available meanings as part of the story to complex layers of more hidden meanings **sub-text and plot**).

Figure 4.1: Key components of a drama event in process drama

Meaning making

Meaning making is at the centre of the activity. The meanings can be mainly personal, the personal in the social, or mainly social. In an alternative version of the little drama of the mother and child, the mother could be irritable with the child from the start. The drama could be refocused to look at her parenting skills or lack of them and the lack of parenting she had herself. The drama could focus on what makes a good parent and what is lacking in her psychological make-up. This could be seen as mainly personal. In another version, it could be focused on the language she chooses to use. If she says 'Children should do as they are told', it would be possible to focus on how ideology is passed on through language and we are then focusing more on the social. I tried to shape our example as one of the personal in the social or, as I quoted Bolton writing earlier, 'To help the student understand himself and the world he lives in' (Bolton, 1976: 1). Again, my preference would be to see this as a dialectical process of exploring the personal in the social and the social in the personal. The mother's positive attitude to her child is gradually being eroded by the economic situation she is in.

If meaning making is at the centre of the drama activity then Dorothy Heathcote's five levels of meaning are a key area of theory, variously called levels of explanation (Gillham, 1988; Gillham, 1997); levels of commitment

(Heathcote and Bolton, 1995); and AMIMS, action, motivation, investment, model and stance (Gee, 2011). I prefer to call them layers of meaning.

Five layers of meaning

Heathcote developed this extremely helpful tool over a number of years but never wrote it up. Gillham (1988; 1997) was the first to do so and elaborate on its usefulness. Heathcote argued that there were at least five major levels in an action: the action itself; its motivation; what was invested in the action; from where it was learned; and its universal dimension or what it revealed about the stance of the participant or, in a more immediately useable form, how life should or should not be.

If the five levels are applied to our small drama, it might look like this. For the child:

ACTION	What is done	Tying a shoe lace
MOTIVATION	Immediate reason	To keep the shoe on
INVESTMENT	Why it is so important/ what's at stake	I want to be grown up
MODEL	Where learned from (positive/negative model)	All the other kids at school can do it
LIFE-VIEW	How life should or should not be	How independent can young people be allowed to be?

For the mother:

ACTION	What is done	Encouraging her child to hurry up
MOTIVATION	Immediate reason	To get to the supermarket
INVESTMENT	Why it is so important/ what's at stake	Whether or not we eat well this week
MODEL	Where learned from (positive/negative model)	The bitter experience of getting into debt
LIFE-VIEW	How life should or should not be	Is it possible to be the parent you'd like to be given the sort of society we live in?

To take another example, imagine a sequence of actions. A young girl is carrying a cup of tea. She is young enough to need to put it down as she opens the door so as not to spill it. She picks it up and goes into the room where her father stands looking out of the window. He has just come in from work. She crosses to him. He turns. She holds out the tea. He takes it and smiles. He is pleased. The major action of bringing father a cup of tea could be set out as follows.

ACTION	What is done	Bringing a drink
MOTIVATION	Immediate reason	Father always has a drink when he comes in from work
INVESTMENT	Why it is so important/ what's at stake	I want to be loved
MODEL	Where learned from (positive/negative model)	Mummy makes daddy a drink and he loves her
LIFE-VIEW	How life should or should not be	Children should/should not have to be the 'ideal' child to be loved

One of the key things the chart enables the teacher to do is quickly assess where the student is at in terms of the significance of the action. Every child can do levels one and two. The child goes into the bank with a gun and says 'Hands up'; the action, and the immediate reason for pointing the gun is wanting some money. But to take it to the next level of the action 'What's at stake?' is a quantum leap. Now we are into the child inventing a background and motivations: 'My mother is dying of a rare illness and I need to get money urgently to send her to the United States for treatment'. Then into 'Where was this learned from?' – perhaps the television. And then to the key areas of exploration: how life should or should not be.

Gillham (1997) added to the theory by moving the five layers firmly into the area of the social. The five layers became: the action; individual consciousness of the action; the social (class) relation of the action; the historical or the individual in the social in the historical; and finally all these in the universal (15).

Gee (2011) has these levels as Action and then describes the next levels as Psychological, Sociological, Historical and Philosophical (25). She seems to indicate this is with Heathcote's approval but this is not clear.

Putting into practice the five layers of meaning and the components of making drama

An exercise I have found useful is to ask students to take a piece of narrative and restructure it as drama. The students in this example could range from older teenagers to students in initial teacher education to teachers on in-service courses. It begins to give them practice in finding dramatic actions that have significance and also begins to develop the complex skills the drama teacher, and, later in their development, their students themselves need in order to make drama. The exercise involves the restructuring of story into drama. Drama manuals that suggest that pupils can act out a story, in my view, take pupils in entirely the wrong direction. Story and drama are different art forms and have different constraints to actualization. The exercise also acts as a stimulus for them to begin consciously using the components of the art form (see Figure 4.1 above).

The narrative extract is from Jeffrey Masson's *Against Therapy* (1990). Masson was a psychotherapist who underwent psychotherapy for 20 years and found he was basically the same as when he started. He gave up both being a therapist and having therapy and wrote the book. He examines every form of therapy available at the time and finds them wanting. His final recommendation is for people to form self-help groups: to me this feels a bit like the blind leading the blind. The following extract is taken from his visit to the Bellevue clinic in Kreuzlingen, Switzerland. It had recently closed but the son of the founder of the clinic allowed him access to the archives where there were thousands of files containing the case histories of every patient who had been in the clinic between 1875 and its closure in 1975. He looked only at the case studies of women who were there between 1880 and 1900. The following is an extract from Masson's book:

> A common scenario, as revealed by the case histories, was the following. A young woman is told by her father (from whom she is somewhat distanced) that he is taking her to visit family members in Switzerland. On the way, the train stops at the rather desolate railway station of Kreuzlingen. It is a quiet winter day. The woman looks out of the window, notices the bleak trees, the stillness of this little place, the streets bare of people, the silent buildings. She sees the dark lake and the mist, and remembers that people call it romantic. Nothing could happen here. (Is it any wonder one patient wrote, 'Nothing exists here,' and another, 'I was hoping it was a bad dream – that it would go away, that I would wake

up'?) She shudders, glad that she comes from Berlin, or Munich, or Vienna. Her father calls her out of the train and introduces her to a man she has never seen: 'Herr Doktor Binswanger.' The father looks embarrassed, shuffles his feet, then abruptly turns away and boards the train, saying, as he leaves: 'Go with him.' This is no vacation; this is her destination. She has been brought, by trickery, to a clinic for hysterical women, a sanatorium for *Nervenkranke*, those ill in their nerves. Binswanger knows little about her. But solely by virtue of her having been brought to him, he 'knows' she is sick, suffering, hysterical. The looks she gives her father in parting makes the diagnosis easy: This young woman is suffering from moral insanity. That is, in the opinion of her family and her doctors, there is nothing wrong with her intellect, or her senses, yet she cannot live like other women. She wants too much, she has too many ideas, she is too independent. She does not know what is best for her. She does not know what correct behaviour is. She is morally insane.

Binswanger was much taken by the term invented by the English doctor. It fit his patients well. What was wrong with them was that they were morally insane. There were so many of them and there seemed to be more all the time. He could barely cope. He had to hire assistants, distinguished doctors like himself.

(Masson, 1990: 67–8)

This was the period just before Rosa Luxemburg became active. It was a period of progressive ideas, of women's emancipation and women becoming more independent: socialism was in the air. There must have been many young women who no longer wanted just to do what their fathers expected of them. They may even have begun to ride bicycles and, heaven forbid, started sitting astride when riding a horse. Masson quotes from an abridged letter to Binswanger in 1894:

Dear Doctor: On the morning of the 11th I shall come to Constanz directly from Innsbruck. I would appreciate it if you could send somebody to meet us since I do not know my way around. My daughter and I are in mourning. She is a tall, slender girl, somewhat taller than I am, very pretty, with black eyes. I will be wearing a hat and shall carry an umbrella with a golden handle in my right hand so that you will be able to recognize me. My daughter does not know that I intend to leave her there. I will tell her that she and

I are going to stay in a *Pension* so that we can rest. Everything will
then fall into place. Sincerely yours, ...

(Masson, 1990: 67)

Masson goes on to describe some of the case studies: young women who
arrived in the full bloom of youth only to be discharged forty years later
straight into an old people's home; other cases where incest may have been
present and it was better for the father to lock his daughter away; and
another case where the daughter showed lesbian tendencies and was shut
away for life.

Working in small groups the students create a short piece of drama to
present to each other with a dramatic action at its centre, thus changing the
narrative structure into a drama structure. It is to be set in the station where
that fateful handover takes place. All the members of the group must take
part. Each group will need to justify the five layers in the action by naming
them and describing the intended outcomes. It is possible to let the students
do whatever they think will make a piece of theatre to present to the others.
This will allow a diagnosis of their present level of skills. Most often the
drama is all words with a minimal action or it re-tells the whole of the event
that is recounted in the extract. Those watching are asked to pick out the
central action and its meanings and it is surprising how difficult this becomes.
It also becomes difficult to use the five layers of meaning once they have to
use them to create an action.

There can also be many clear demonstrations of potential dramatic
action once the creativity of the participants is stimulated. What is the
weather like? Is it raining? Do people have umbrellas? Or, what else is on
the platform? Is there a flower stall and a flower seller? Are there porters or
station workers present? And so on. Once the idea of imagery in the context
has taken hold and the realization that theatre is not predominantly words but
made up of actions, images and words (in that order of priority) then things
can begin to happen. One example that comes to mind is of the father who
pretends reconciliation and takes his daughter to the flower stall to buy her
a bouquet of flowers and then walks down the platform towards the doctor
and his assistants, creating the image of a father walking his daughter down
the aisle to be married and then handing her over to imprisonment, which
must have happened to many a young woman in an arranged marriage. Then
what she does with the flowers when she realizes what is happening gives
plenty of scope for inventive action.

The whole exercise can be worked at in stages if that is more likely
to help the participants: exercises to begin to protect into the role of people

in that highly formalized class structure, allowing them to approach the sort of register they might have used with each other; focusing possible central meanings; different images that can be created and so on.

It can be useful just to focus on simple actions rather than trying to put together a whole scene that is likely to be dominated by storyline. For example, the daughter sanely questioning her father while she is being restrained. He is at the carriage window and slowly and firmly pulls up the window with the leather strap. Or the girl, who is being held firmly by her father, simply taking her hand away, which possibly takes some effort. These two examples of action could be illustrated as follows:

ACTION	Father winding up window
MOTIVATION	Train has to go
INVESTMENT	Final shutting out of daughter from his life
MODEL	His own father
LIFE-VIEW	The young who will not stay gratefully in the nest should be thrown out

ACTION	Release of hand from father by girl
MOTIVATION	Train has to go
INVESTMENT	She will stand alone
MODEL	Not to be like father
LIFE-VIEW	Not the sort of autonomy needed by children

Re-working this situation as a 'living through' experience

One of the most important areas of theory is how to embed the components of process drama as art into improvisations set up by the drama teacher so there can be a dimension of a 'lived through' experience but with no support of teacher in role. 'Living through' is again one of those strange terms. Everything has to be lived through but the term carries with it a sense of the unplanned, of exploration, of the experiences that might come from this form of involvement. Again, the *metaxis* dimension means the part that is 'I am making it happen' involves a dimension of consciously working in the art form. The more the student knows about how the art form operates, the more those dimensions can be worked for. In the following drama event the participants are supplied with a tight structure within which they can explore what lies between them. Let us take the above relationship between father and daughter and rework it as a pair's improvisation. Let us go back to the imagined incident that led up to the father's decision to have the child committed, to create a possible final straw that broke the camel's back.

I am imagining the students have all explored the group exercise of the handover at the station and now are asked to work in pairs. I am presuming that in each pair there is a female who will take the role of the daughter. First the context is given. The original text is of a German family but it could be any big European city during the last twenty years of the nineteenth century, including late Victorian and into Edwardian England. I ask them to imagine an upper-middle-class family. It is the time when those who can afford it have their own horse and carriage. I describe one of those big city houses where you can drive into an inner courtyard. Here there is a stable for the horse and carriage. It is an early autumn evening, a night when the father has arranged a dinner for important guests, maybe people he wants to influence for some reason. The scene takes place in the stable. Outside on the first floor gas lights have already been lit and the first guests are arriving. There is the sound of socializing, voices, laughter maybe. In the stable is the daughter – in work clothes. She is cleaning the tack (the horse's harness) by the light of a lamp. She has decided that the next day, when they are due to visit relatives in the country, she will drive the carriage. She cannot see why they need a servant to drive them. It is only for show and why shouldn't a woman drive a carriage? She has dismissed the stable hand. The pair, father and daughter, are asked to set up the scene. The lamp is shown simply by a circle of paper placed on the floor. To pick up the lantern a person just needs to mime picking it up from above the circle of paper. The circle of paper simply shows where the lamp is positioned. It may be worth spending a little time finding what will work as the leather harness. For example, the strap of a leather handbag might well work whereas a plastic belt would totally disrupt the visual aesthetic. If nothing is to hand then completely miming the action will be better. The daughter is terrified of the dark. Maybe as a child, as a punishment, she was locked in a cellar in the dark and had rats crawling on her. The father has told her she is to take her recently dead mother's place as hostess for the night's party. After dinner she will play the piano or sing. The father has bought her a suitable dress for the occasion, which lies unworn upstairs on her bed. He is determined to get her to come and take her rightful place. He has to do this carefully and subtly. He cannot raise his voice or cause her to shout or scream. It would cause a scandal. They are asked to make a still image so that all the pairs can start the scene at the same time: the girl in the act of cleaning the harness; the father standing in the doorway. He is sure he could as a final resort get her to comply simply by taking away the lamp but this would risk a scene.

Then the five layers can be introduced as questions. The pairs are warned that they should stay in their still images and just think of their answers to the questions in silence.

Of the daughter: What do you do? Of the father: What do you intend to do?

Why do you do it? What is the immediate reason you do it?

Why is it so important? What's at stake here for you?

Where did you learn this? (A very interesting one for the daughter to invent.)

How does this capture how you think life should or should not be?

Then all the pairs are set off together. They can find their own moment to finish. Those who finish before the others are just to sit and talk it over quietly. I have known pairs, totally immersed, still going strong after twenty minutes of improvising. The dead mother tended to play a prominent part in the exchange introduced from both sides. Also the growing rights of women in opposition to the dominant patriarchy and the developing sense of class struggle appearing socially. These sorts of comments tended to come from adults involved in the improvisation and it had been devised for them. Clearly for a group of teenage students more background work would be needed to enable them to have material to draw on.

If the event is analysed the major components in Figure 4.1, above, have been laid in. A **context** has been set up: the stable and outside that the dinner party and outside that the rapid development of modernity very much dominated by a patriarchal society whose value system is self-advancement. It has **pre-text**: the important (to the father) social evening that has been arranged; for the daughter, her plans for the next day. There are **roles** and each role has an **objective**, which is set up so that together they make **counter-objectives**. The father has to get her to agree to come and take her dead mother's place: to clean up and put on her lovely new dress. The daughter is determined that she will no longer play the stereotypical role. This is her extreme bid for freedom. The father's preliminary **attitude** is one of treading carefully. The daughter's is likely to be wary. The way they each work to pursue their objective creates the **tension** of the scene. There is a **constraint** in that the father cannot just drag her screaming from the stable and this slows down **time**. This allows time to **focus** the **layers of meaning**: she is fighting for her independence and is forced to try something that to the average citizen of the time would seem outrageous. As they work for their objectives they have available **objects, images, body language** and **words**, particularly the language register appropriate to the time. The more experience, skill and knowledge of how drama works, the more resources they will have to draw on. The less they have the more protection into the roles they will need. The situation has the potential to help them experience from inside the thematic dimensions of **sub-text**. The **event**, persuading the daughter to take her mother's place, has all the potential complexities of a Strindberg play: the exploration of Oedipal relationships and sexual tensions; love/hate relationships; the power struggle between the genders; the possibility of emotional blackmail; the struggle between a humanizing and an inhuman agenda. The father has the threat of picking up the lantern [object]and testing the waters of taking the light away. In fact this is a horrific potential **dramatic action**. How could any loving father threaten an act that would traumatize his daughter? These may seem extreme or exaggerated claims to make but as students become more familiar with this sort of work, and develop the ability to submit to the experience they are also making, then it is possible to reach for these themes.

It is easy for the experienced drama teacher to see at a glance who is 'in', working at being in role, and who is 'out', working at it from outside as a staged event. Of course, I have also experienced those who have a real difficulty finding a way in. Where this is strongly present it is usually because I have not done enough to protect them into role, particularly into the language register and the family/social mores of the time.

It might be worth underlining this as an example where the students can 'live through' a situation *without* the teacher in role, provided that the teacher has made sure the components, without which the form will not work successfully, are made available for the students to employ. With this heavy teacher structuring, it is possible for students new to drama to have success. It may be useful to set out another example where the components are put in place by the drama teacher and the students then engage and explore a situation but with each participant having only part of the information. This is a well-known strategy, and the impact is increased by adding the components. When the teacher makes these available to the students it is possible for them to engage with the situation significantly without the long building into role that could be necessary for a more complex process drama. As the students become more experienced they can be made increasingly aware of how the art form is structured.

Using hidden information

The following short drama situation was invented for Palestinian teachers who had never tried drama before. I started with short pairs exercises where each pair are neighbours in various situations: good friends discussing problems they are having with teenage sons; one neighbour finding a way to tell the other that she had been gossiped about; one neighbour asking another for a favour and so on.

Then they are asked to form pairs **A** and **B**. All they are told as shared information is that neighbour **B** has moved recently to live next door to **A**'s family. **B** has not had time to get to know the **A** family very well but has met and talked with all the family members and likes them. **B** knows that there have been politically active members of the family and several of the family members have spent time in Israeli prisons. (This would be the norm in Palestine.) **B**'s family is not politically active and does not want to get involved with activism and is asked to invent the reasons for this while waiting for **A** to arrive. There is some past experience that means they definitely want no involvement but of course **B** supports the struggle for independence. Neighbour **A** is the son or daughter in her late teens or early 20s. S/he lives with her brothers/sisters and her parents. S/he is shortly going to arrive at neighbour **B**'s house with a large heavy suitcase. If **A** is a daughter and **B** a man it could be seen as improper to invite her in so they may have to talk on chairs in the garden or yard. If they are of the same gender then there is no problem.

While **B** is asked to set up his/her house, signed by at least two chairs, **A** is given separate information. His/her family are all away visiting and looking after a very sick relative. S/he has been left to look after the house and the suitcase, which s/he has been told contains important family papers and deeds to property inside Israel. It is extremely heavy and a great struggle to move. The father has the key and has taken it with him. Now s/he has been told to come to say her goodbyes to her relative whose health has deteriorated. **A** has been told to see if the neighbour will keep the suitcase safely until their return. **A** presumes it is the truth that there are only masses of family papers in the case but cannot check. The case has never been opened in **A**'s presence. It will be important to observe any usual courtesies before moving on to the suitcase. However, **A** has to get a bus/taxi as soon as possible.

Many of the improvisations went on for some considerable time. Some of the Bs accepted care of the suitcase; some of them found very respectful and careful ways of declining. This latter tended to cause some distress to the As and this, in turn, sometimes led to a change of heart. The discussion afterwards centred around questions such as: Should we always help our neighbours? Can we always do that? In our society can we always be as we would like to be? Would that be possible in any society? Where does lack of trust in another come from?

The components could be set out as follows:

Pre-text	The family background and present circumstances
Context	The daily problem of living in an occupied country
Roles	Language register and rules of behaviour within reach
Attitudes	They like each other and get on together but do not know each other well
Constraint	The key is not available to show contents of the suitcase but there is the need to catch a bus
Action in event	Taking suitcase to leave at neighbour's house
Object	Heavy suitcase – what's really in it?
Focusing meaning	To trust neighbour or not
Counter-objectives	One neighbour wanting to leave suitcase, the other not sure – producing ...
Tension/dilemma and slowing down time	In order to provide a space to explore meanings

One reason for choosing this example is the different cultural setting. There is always the challenge of finding just that context for the drama that students can relate to. After many years of visiting Palestine and teaching there I was still an outsider to the intimacies of the culture, so I was taking a risk with my material. There seem to me to be parallels here for any teacher. Process drama, in fact any drama, is always context specific. If the teacher is working in a classroom where 90 per cent of the students are of a different ethnicity, they are working in a different immediate cultural setting to the teacher in a white middle-class catchment area, although the larger social context remains the same in both cases. And this would alter country to country and area to area. The teacher has to tune in to that cultural setting as closely as possible. I remember teaching a workshop session for Palestinian teachers and right in the middle of an improvisation one of the women suddenly ran out in enormous haste and with an air of anxiety. Everyone else ignored her sudden departure. I followed suit. In the lunch hour I was able to ask her if she was alright. She was full of apologies and explained that her husband was in prison and there was a mobile phone that had been smuggled in that the prisoners took turns in using. This was extremely difficult and the moment had to be seized when it was possible to use it with less chance of being discovered. She had received the signal that he could speak to her and so rushed out to snatch that precious moment. Everyone else understood what was happening except for me. But this will happen to any teacher in a strange environment.

The relevant areas of theory that could be of use here are: secondary symbolism; the angle of connection; relevance and significance; the play for class and the play for teacher. These are all areas that are predominantly the sole responsibility of the teacher.

Relevance and significance

All process drama should obviously have relevance and significance, but how to decide what is relevant to a particular class, of a particular age, in a particular area of the country, mixed or same gender, with a lot or little drama experience, plus a host of other variables such as space available, curriculum expectations of school and students and so on, all makes for a complicated process of decision making for the teacher. Furthermore, unless the students 'buy' into the topic and enjoy it, their engagement is likely to be formal rather than real. This is encapsulated in Gillham's phrase 'play for class, play for teacher' (Gillham, 1974). Gavin Bolton drew attention to Gillham's phrase in his first book on drama in education (Bolton, 1979: 51) and it entered the theory of DiE from there. The play for class contains the students' 'kicks'; where they can find enjoyment, fun, excitement, and deep interest and commitment. Play for teacher contains the important dimensions of human experience the teacher wants the class to engage with and the knowledge of how to work in the art form to explore those areas. Sometimes teachers see these as separate areas; first work for the interest and fun and then find the significance. I think it is important to remember they are congruent: synchronous and not diachronic. They need to be interwoven from the start.

To arrive at the choice of material that contains all these features requires a finely tuned ear. This is where the other two areas of theory have their uses: secondary symbolism and the angle of connection. Again it is Bolton who is the first to refer to these two areas: secondary symbolism (Bolton, 1979: 24–6) and angle of connection (61). He refers to the latter as finding an 'angle within a topic' (60). Angle of connection is my phrasing of the same area.

Secondary symbolism and the angle of connection

Why do very young children sit enthralled by fairy tales such as *Hansel and Gretel*, *Little Red Riding Hood* and *Cinderella*? Take *Hansel and Gretel*.

Psychologists tell us that one of the primary fears of young children is of being abandoned (see, for example, Wolman, 1978). In *Hansel and Gretel*, lo and behold, the child's worst fears are realized: parents do abandon their children. No wonder they sit half-hidden under the bedclothes as the brother and sister are trapped by the witch (the other side of a mother who can suddenly lose her temper and deliver a slap) and Hansel is locked in a cage to be fattened up and Gretel is turned into a servant. When they return home with the witch's jewels, solving the problem of their parents' poverty, they have separated out and become young adults able to deal with the world on their own. Little Red Riding Hood is sent out into the world on an errand without an adult to guide her. It is as though it is the very first time a child has to go into town to the shops on her own when she is really too young to do so. This is a possible area of attraction of which the child is not consciously aware. And, of course, the world is full of dangers. Cinderella is filled with longing for parental love, bullied by her stepsisters, and the target of sibling rivalry. She is neglected and feels unloved. Whether one agrees or not with her salvation at the hands of a handsome prince is not the point. What is of interest is the unconscious/subconscious level of engagement with the stories. On the surface level children respond to the primary symbolism of these fantasy figures: young people in danger, having adventures. On a deeper level, the level of secondary symbolism, they respond to the deep content contained in the stories, content they could not articulate. It remains at a subliminal level. Bettelheim (1976) offers useful interpretations of these fairy tales in his book *The Uses of Enchantment*, although I find his approach rather too Freudian.

The demand on the teacher is to be able to find areas of potential secondary symbolism, subject matter that will attract on a deeper subconscious level, and then find material or situations that can be structured to find a way into that material: the angle of connection. If the choice of area has come from the students then the theory helps to guess at what might be informing the choice.

I once worked with a group of adults with learning difficulties who spent the days at a centre but went home in the evenings. When I asked them what they would like to explore they all chose *Cinderella*. The oldest in the group was well over 40, so why were they so interested in *Cinderella*? I guess it was because they never get to go to the ball. When the family went to the pub or out for a social evening they were often left at home, the more capable to babysit. We set up a drama where they were left to babysit, with strict instructions not to leave the house because of the sleeping child upstairs.

We enacted various scenarios where this was put to the test, for example an emergency that meant s/he had to decide whether to leave the house to get help or stay in the house with a growing problem. They all ended up being the toast of the pub after they had solved the problems.

On another occasion I was teaching some lessons in a secondary school after I had moved into higher education, just to keep my hand in with young people. On the way from the staff room to the class, one of the teachers said to me under her breath, 'They've given you the worst class in the school. Good luck!' I was left on my own, as I had requested. I welcomed the class at the door, a mixed-gender group of 13- and 14-year-olds. We settled down into a circle and I asked them their names. They all answered in a friendly enough way. It was the point when they were assessing the new teacher, weighing up the lie of the land. I asked them what they would like to do some drama about and they quickly and unanimously chose *St Trinian's*. The film, which had recently been on television, is about a totally anarchic girls' school where the girls were more likely to be running a betting shop than doing curriculum maths. It was a clever choice. It meant they could legitimately be the worst class in the worst school in the country and if they did not like me or what we were doing, they had licence to cause chaos.

We turned the school into a co-educational one with a new name. It would be a mistake to stay too close to the original. I decided the only way forward was to go for a very tight structure. We started with me in role as the class teacher writing on the board. While my back was turned they created mayhem, throwing paper planes across the class, flicking paper, moving around and so on. They were very good at inventing what could go on behind teacher's back but the second I turned around they all had to be sitting at their desks as good as gold and quiet as mice. They enjoyed the game but whenever I turned round I caught someone out, not yet back in place. I tried giving more and more warnings about when I was about to turn around but I still caught someone every time no matter how much warning I gave them. On one of the occasions when they were causing maximum chaos, planes flying everywhere, I noticed the head and deputy head looking in over the top of the frosted panes in the door. They exchanged knowing glances as if to say they suspected that a lecturer would make a mess of it. They moved off satisfied.

However, the class and I were enjoying ourselves. They had by this time told me that they were the worst class in the school and the drama had graduated to a chemistry lesson where they had set up a whisky distillery. I was now the government inspector who, when he entered the laboratory, was to find an apparently orderly lesson with all the students able to explain the legitimate experiment they were doing. I still caught them out every time, whisky bottles in full view, labels left lying on the table. At the end of the lesson, as they filed out, I said goodbye by name to those I had remembered. They immediately put me straight, 'Oh no sir! Those aren't our real names. We gave you false ones for a laugh at the start of the lesson.' In real life they could be as sharp as they needed or wanted to be but in the drama they were caught out every time. I never solved that contradiction.

In a later lesson we did one of those television programmes where a successful personality is interviewed and people from their past come in and tell anecdotes about them. One of the personalities they invented was a past pupil of their anarchic school who had become an extremely successful self-made millionaire. He had set up a whisky distillery and made a fortune. They enjoyed bringing on the head teacher (me as teacher in role) to make him squirm and quiz him about why he had seen only the bad points of the pupil when he was at school. It led into very good discussions about the role of education and what sort of school they would like and what would make the most useful curriculum.

The secondary symbolism was easily perceived. They were both proud of being the worst class and strongly resentful. It gave them some status but meant they were always being put down. The two dramas had enabled them to articulate and get in touch with these concerns in an indirect way, yet they would have been unlikely to be able to explain the reason for their choices of drama situations. It is a subconscious association. An experienced teacher could have worked out this connection without the theory, but the theory is extremely useful as the symptoms are commonly found if the class is really excited about the choice of material. It is even more useful when the teacher is initiating the subject matter.

Sequencing and internal coherence

The drama teacher is always inventing structures for the drama lesson and for the drama within it. Key to the planning are the notions of sequencing and internal coherence. It might be useful to start with an example where each of these is missing. If we imagine that the drama teacher is asking the class to improvise scenes related to *Romeo and Juliet* he might ask them:

1. To be the townspeople after the first fracas between the two families at the start of the play and to be talking about the damage done to their market stalls and their goods, and what they should do about it.

Then:

2. To imagine they are members of Capulet's household discussing who won, who was hurt, who did the best 'swashing blows', what damage has been done physically and mentally and so on.

Not only is it an impossible task to just ask them 'to be' any role, especially one that is so distant from their own lives, but the sequence of the structure is not internally coherent. The students have done their best to conjure up the world of the stallholders and then the teacher asks them to switch from that internal state to a completely different one. The structure follows the coherence of the teacher's plan. He wants to contrast the attitudes of the different groups of people caught up in this feud. If this lesson is now restructured to take account of the need to preserve internal coherence, it might start to look something like the following:

1. The teacher is now at the black or whiteboard and the class are out of role and grouped in front of the teacher. He starts to draw the outline of the imagined centre of Verona. This could start with the prompt from the teacher that there seems to be a central square where the stallholders had their market. The map of the square is negotiated with the class – would there be buildings round the square? What might they be? The class might suggest a church, with wide steps leading up to the entrance; a fountain in the middle; rich merchants' houses and shops round the square; narrow alleys leading into the square from each side; the place for the stalls and so on.

2. Again out of role the teacher might initiate a discussion about what the stallholders might do about the constant overturning of their stalls and the damage to their goods: they could be ruined; there is no such thing as insurance; and they are so vulnerable compared to the rich merchants' warehouses and stores. All this talking about the stallholders is in the third person. The students might suggest '*They* could post lookouts', '*They* could hire some ex-soldiers to guard them' and so on. (The teacher here would be looking out in case anyone started saying '*We* could …', which can sometimes happen as they start to empathize with the role. Then the teacher makes a mental note that that particular student is 'in'.)

3. The teacher has prepared lots of small blank cards and with available felt tip pens asks the class to write down as many types of stall they can think of that might be in the market. They start to write such things as: baker's goods; vegetables; fruit; shoes; cobbler; fabrics; wine and so on. It does

not matter if the same stalls appear more than once. Each student aims to produce three or four. These are then all set out in the middle of the floor and the students are invited to take one.

4. They are asked to find a partner and spend a couple of minutes helping each other decide what is on the stall of that stallholder. (Not *my* stall but *their* stall.)

5. The teacher gathers them back round the board and starts to write a petition that they might have written: 'We the humble citizens of Verona beg …' and the rest of the petition is written with the suggestions from the class. Almost inevitably by this stage someone will start using the first person. 'I think we should be more definite and not go begging for help.' 'But we don't have any power or influence and can only beg.' The teacher just notes who and how many are slipping into role and at some point might also slip into the first person.

The teacher has started by building the role perspective of one role rather than two. If the teacher wanted to switch later to build the role perspective of the Capulets, there would have to be a bridging activity that did not break the internal coherence. An example of such an activity might be anticipating how the letter was received, starting with how it would be delivered to the Prince (TiR), and then a stage where the townspeople imagined how the courtiers would respond by building their actual world. I would argue that this is a structure where each stage of the sequencing prepares for the next stage and where each step is internally coherent for the students. It is also an example of protecting into role, which I elaborate on in a separate section.

To recapitulate:

Sequencing is the step-by-step staging of tasks by the teacher, either pre-planned or negotiated with the students, which is *externally* observable and involves making sure that each stage of the work prepares for the next and that the next links to the previous. Each stage or step is a part of the whole that holds the central concerns and develops the context, circumstances, dilemmas and investment in relation to the major events of the drama.

Internal coherence is achieved by ensuring that the mental dimensions conjured up in one stage of the work are compatible with the next. It is the internal logic experienced by the students as they go through a sequence of activities. All the parts are logically organized, consistent with each other and comprehensible to the receiver because the internal structure they exist within develops without dissonant factors for the participants. Teachers often think of sequencing in terms of storyline and can fall into the trap of building external coherence (i.e. logical for the teacher only) rather than internal coherence (where each step builds coherently for the student). If the teacher knows the arrival point, then planning can be seen as 'backfilling', i.e. to provide all the necessary stages for this moment to be arrived at and engaged with authentically in role. This is sequencing that has to build internally coherently for the child. Heathcote and Bolton (1995: 117–68) give an extended lesson structure setting out each external activity and its internal coherence.

As well as inventing or co-inventing structures, the drama teacher has to decide on the frame of entry into the drama events most useful for the students.

Frame distance

Dorothy Heathcote developed her own version of frame from Goffman's *Frame Analysis* (1974). I noted earlier that Heathcote moved from her early interest in being in the event to being in a frame distance from the event. She developed a hierarchy of frames each one further removed from being in the event. The chart in Figure 4.2 is taken from an early workshop handout, which was not to my knowledge published in this format, but is identical to later published versions.

Although my preference is for the participants to be in the event, one of the interesting features of frame distance is that in any of the frames it can also become an event in itself. I remember being in a workshop with Heathcote in the 1980s and she had chosen the story of the Good Samaritan as the event. We were in role as Roman soldiers whose job it was to keep the peace on the road between Jerusalem and Jericho. Heathcote was in role as the centurion in charge. She berated us, in fact tore us to shreds, for our lax guarding of the road. The frame rapidly became a very strong experience in its own right about what it must have been like to be a legionnaire in a dusty, dry, foreign land. Frame therefore seems to me a very useful tool for the teacher using process drama. It does not have to become a distanced role but it is useful to know what the relationship is to the main event. As we approach any event in real life we take a particular relationship to it. If we are going to a pub to relax with friends we know the dress code, the language registers likely to be appropriate, and we adjust our interests, attitudes and behaviour according to our general cultural understanding of those situations and our reading of the particular event we are attending. If we are going to a staff meeting we adjust all these areas accordingly.

General role function in relation to frame distance

Each frame distance provides students with a different, specific responsibility, interest, attitude and behaviour in relation to an event.

1. Participant ... *I am in the event*

2. Guide... ... ... *I show you how the event was; I was there*

3. Agent... ... ... *I must re-enact the event so that it may be understood*

4. Authority... ... *I must reconstruct the meaning of the event because it has occurred*

5. Recorder... ... *I clarify for those in the future so they may know the truth of the event*

6. Press... ... ... *I was not there, but I provide a commentary as to why I think the event happened*

7. Researcher... *I research the event for those who live now*

8. Critic... ... ... *I critique/interpret the event as event*

9. Artist... ... ... *I transform the event*

(After Heathcote, 1980)

Figure 4.2: General role function in relation to frame distance

I prefer to work outwards from social situations to an understanding of frame rather than to try to work from a chart. This can be shown in a workshop situation quite easily. The teacher puts a couple of chairs in the central workshop space and asks the students to form a circle round them. The chairs represent a nasty car crash; the cars are wrecked and the driver and passenger injured. It has taken place at a crossroads in town that is a black spot for accidents. The students are asked to come forward in pairs, as people who are around the crash, and say who they are: passers-by, local residents, two teenagers on the way to college, police officers, medics, two relatives who have been contacted and so on. Then each pair is asked to exchange a few words. It becomes clear that each is in a different frame and shows different **attitudes, responsibilities, behaviour** and **language genres**. It is possible to order them according to the frame chart (Figure 4.2). For example:

1. driver blaming other driver – **participant**

2. witness in court case – **guide**

3. solicitor for one of drivers, making model of accident – **agent**

4. judge in court – **authority**

5. local resident getting information to record exactly what happens in each of these accidents – **recorder**

6. reporter creating sensational newspaper headline – **press**

7. children taking the initiative to research newspaper files of the event, which give many different reasons for why accidents happen there – **researcher**

8. priest blaming the pace and pressure of modern life – **critic**

9. TiE company reworking how the lives of these people have been affected to make a programme for primary schools – **artist**.

However, it is worth bearing in mind that each frame can become an event in itself. I find that following the chart too rigidly can sometimes be limiting. If we take another example it should be possible to see that each frame could be developed into its own process drama. I give only the briefest outline of the situation, which I hope will be enough to demonstrate my point.

Imagine that the drama is about famine relief that never arrived. Following the frame distance chart the drama activities might look like the following:

1. **Participant** – I am in the event.

The whole group works to be in the event. They are to make three still images. They are the people waiting for the famine relief, starving, weak. They may have walked for days to get to the distribution point. They have been waiting for days.

First still image: one by one the participants come into the centre and make an individual still image, stating who they are. For example, one is an elderly person who has walked twenty miles; one is a mother; another is that mother's child. We see the mother readjust her image to accommodate and comfort the starving child. This continues until all are in the still image.

Second still image: an aid worker who has come to make an announcement. The participants readjust their images.

Third still image: after they have just been told the food convoy will not arrive that day.

2. **Guide** – I was there. I show you how the event was.

In pairs, both are aid workers, one explains to the other how it was to have been the aid worker who kept bringing the bad news. It is told with demonstrating gestures, as in an anecdote.

3. **Agent** – I must re-enact the event so that it may be understood.

The whole group are people mounting an exhibition. In groups of four they make photographs of the appalling consequences when famine relief goes wrong. For example, one group might make a photograph of normal children of the country at play and then a photograph of children when the famine relief has not arrived. One half of the group looks at the other half's still images and *vice versa*. They then choose which photographs to put in which order.

4. **Authority** – I must reconstruct the meaning of the event because it has occurred.

The whole group are going to be a UN official enquiry team. It would work well if the whole class quickly worked together with the teacher to make up the background information.

The outline of the country could quickly be mapped out on a black or whiteboard. This could include the main features of the terrain, mountain areas, deserts, main roads, dirt tracks, any airports, seaports, population size, economy, reason for famine; estimates of the amount of food aid needed, for example, thousands of kilos of grain in 20 kilo sacks and other sorts of aid. It would serve as the briefing they would have had before the start of the enquiry. The teacher would be in role as the ground coordinator in charge in the country in question. The aid was sent but so much went missing it turned into a disaster. Corruption is suspected. The students are in role as a UN Board of Enquiry to gather evidence in order to make recommendations, which could range from criminal proceedings to dismissal for negligence or clearing the individual's name.

5. **Recorder** – I clarify for those in the future so they may know the truth of the event.

Working in pairs, one is the recorder who has no views on the event but just takes notes. The other person has been a member of the above UN enquiry team. The recorder's aim is to set down an accurate report of what happened in the enquiry.

6. **Press** – I was not there but provide commentary on what I think happened (always a bias).

In groups of three the students make up the headline and first few lines of articles. They need to decide if they work for a tabloid or broadsheet newspaper.

7. **Researcher** – I research the event for those who live now.

The teacher has made up a set of statistics for pairs to work on as if the statistics had been drawn up by the office in the country concerned. It is part of a report on the crisis that developed. It sets out, for example, the total amount and sorts of aid; the number of lorries available to distribute the aid; the distances to different famine relief centres; a list of dates by which food should have arrived and been distributed; a list of places needing food; dates when food actually arrived and the amounts; the amount of money sent out to spend locally on hiring lorries and jeeps; the amounts of money spent on petrol, salaries and so on; an estimate of the amount of food stolen or corrupted or lost through crashes and so on. Among the figures are things that do not add up. The teacher can take this as far as s/he wants, producing fake and genuine receipts and so on. These could be hard or easy to find depending on the student group. The students are researchers working on this report, which has been accepted at the enquiry without being challenged.

If the students are older and very capable they could divide into groups and devise their own reports and then swap with another group to research them.

8. **Critic** – I critique the event and I must find out what is useful for us now.

In groups of four the students prepare the first three or four minutes of a television exposé programme that will aim to reveal the truth of the failed famine relief as the team sees it.

9. **Artist** – I transform the event.

In groups of four, the students sketch out very briefly the idea for a play by finding a theme, corruption for example, and then work out how it might be opened up in the play. How did an idealist become corrupted and get involved in this massive scandal? They present the outline scenarios to each other.

My argument is that all of these can also be turned into process drama where the participants are in the event. Just two examples make my point. First, I could move away from the actual and use allegory. It could be set in the future with global warming, extreme weather situations, flooding and so on, and those in the drama are trapped and waiting for aid that never comes. Although I have moved it from a famine situation that could actually occur now into one set in the future, both have the participants *in* the event and deal with the same topic. The theme could explore whether or not we should expect to be rescued or should be self-reliant. Aid always comes with a penalty. Or take number six, the newspaper office; it is easy to see how a drama could be developed about selling newspapers versus getting at the truth. In fact, this theme of 'to expose corruption or not' could be played out in almost any of the above situations. The frame has to be present in order to find a way into an event or situation but the role does not have to be in a distanced mode.

Modes of involvement

There are many degrees and forms of involvement, each of which can shift the perspective and experience of the participants. It is important for the drama teacher to have a sense of just how wide this range can be.

The frame from which an event is perceived and entered into was explored above, but this does not determine the mode of involvement of the participants in the event: the levels of thinking/feeling/emotional engagement. The drama activities listed below each aim for a different mode of involvement with the intention of moving from the event to what should be more distanced modes of engagement with it. They are set out rather schematically because of the pressure on space, with a brief commentary in italics following them. I have taken groups of students through each of these in turn and asked them to fill in a chart attempting to capture their level and form of engagement. Sometimes this was done after each mode and sometimes after they were all completed. The categories they were given are shown in Figure 4.3:

Level of emotion	Feeling predominant (not conscious of thought process)	Feeling thoughtfully	Thinking feelingly	Rational thought

Fill in the chart after each activity with numbers 1–5, 5 being the highest.
All boxes can be filled in if there was a level of engagement of each sort.

Figure 4.3: Chart to capture level and form of student engagement

I have not included the actual chart in the text as this seems unnecessary but it is included in the Appendix. It has each activity down the left-hand side with a separate row each for actors/demonstrators in activities three, five and six described below. Emotion is identified as a separate category from thinking/feeling. Although they are related, the mind seems to me to interrogate information in sensory mode which leads to thinking/feeling responses. These can range from intuitive flashes of insight, too fast for rational recognition of the process, to the slow deliberation of conceptual thought. Emotion is not feeling. I can feel or sense that something is wrong without an accompanying emotion, but when I realize that my young child has gone missing, a range of emotions rush in with a mixture of fear, guilt, anxiety and so on. The level of emotional engagement is fairly clear as a descriptor but it is often very difficult to gauge or recognize one's level of emotion in retrospect. I have separated feeling and rational thought. I do recognize, following Best (1992), that feeling is intertwined with thinking, but I have tried to make distinctions between them. At one end of a continuum I put intuitive responses, when one feels something is right, for example, but cannot put it into words. This category is labelled 'feeling predominant'. I have used Walter Benjamin's 'feeling thoughtfully' and 'thinking feelingly', which were his descriptors of art and science respectively, but I am using the terms in a general sense. At the other end of the continuum I placed 'rational thought', where there is little feeling and less emotion. I recognize that more often than not we move up and down the continuum and the categories are intertwined rather than separate. I can be thinking rationally about the structure of this book and just feel something is better than something else without being able to articulate why at the time I felt it or become completely frustrated with myself and go and mow the lawn. The results were surprising and I comment on these after detailing the activities themselves.

Six different modes of involvement

1. The students are asked to take on the role of people in a retirement home:

a) Givens – living on state pension only, or modest pension, and the state supplements payment to the home – not able to afford to own a home any longer – have family (children, grandchildren) who visit seldom – hide feelings – always put on a positive front.

b) Make a small space for room with a few key belongings. Draw these on paper or write on paper what it is – teacher can demonstrate this – and have writing materials handy.

c) Sit in room – write down major achievements in your life.

d) Decide on one internal thing wrong that causes you a problem – may have slight external sign, such as blood flowing away from head when standing, causing attacks of giddiness; pain in back that comes and goes; stiffness of joints in hand, for example – try it out and keep it throughout.

e) Write to son/daughter in role – thanking for card and present to come – acknowledge that you realize they have busy lives and look forward to the present when it comes – cover real feelings.

f) Entry in diary using a metaphor – expressing real feelings.

g) Decide upon another resident to visit – someone you have not yet got to know – both of you have had a birthday recently – decide on a present to take and draw it or write the name of it on paper.

h) Visit neighbour – find out what you talk about – each other's families? the past?

Here there has been a slow and steady protection into role. By the time they reach step 'h' there should be a lot to draw on. The mode of involvement here is being in the event as an elderly person. This would be difficult for teenagers and it was designed for adults, who can make the connection more easily the older they are. It is anticipated that there would be the possibility of a considerable feeling/emotional engagement with the role at certain times. Metaxis is aimed for.

2. There has been a suicide of a resident. Students are asked to put the two sets of personal objects they made previously into just one of the rooms – that of the person who committed suicide. This same pairing then become care workers who work in the home. They have been told to put all the personal belongings into a black bin bag for relatives to collect. The care workers both knew the resident who committed suicide very well. S/he had said 'When I die, I want my clothes to go to Oxfam along with anything else that will sell and the rest of my personal belongings are to be destroyed. Promise!' – and they promised.

a) The two care workers to go into the room. They have been told by management to put all belongings into the bag because the relatives are anxious to have them. They have to find out how they handle this.

This now has the dimension that all the belongings were, in fact, made by the two care workers when in role as residents. At least half of the items will have a strong personal resonance for each of them and the others may have been referred to during the visit. They are, in effect, putting their own prized possessions into the bin bag (or not). It makes the metaxis effect available. It is important that they have an actual black bin bag.

3. The relatives have collected the belongings and claim there are important personal items missing. The Board of Governors of the home has set up an enquiry. Two of the carers volunteer to be the ones brought before the enquiry and the rest of the students, with TiR as chair, set up the Board of Enquiry.

a) The pair is brought in after the committee has had a little time to discuss its approach. They are told that the relatives want to call in the police and start criminal proceedings. The home is accused of negligence and the carers of theft.

TiR has time to prepare the role engagement of the committee. They are members of the local community and if they are not able to contain the situation and find out exactly what has happened their own reputations will be on the line, as well as the reputation of the home itself. There is time for the TiR to prepare the genre of language, attitudes (which may vary), objectives and so on. Metaxis aimed for. Even though this seems like a distanced activity, TiR can make it into a 'living through' event.

4. Out of role, in groups of three, design on paper an 'ideal' home for senior citizens.

Share designs with each other.

This activity was included to break the tension of the activities and to compare the range of responses out of role. It would seem to be the activity furthest removed from the suicide. If possible, large sheets of paper and felt tip pens need to be available for this activity. It is interesting how avidly the students go to this task after having had the above experiences.

5. In groups of four they have to prepare a lecture-demo or video clip to be used by the care home to prepare/train care workers on how to talk to elderly people while helping them to undress for a bath. One of the group, an experienced care worker, acts as a lecturer, explaining and commenting on the recommended procedures. The others, also experienced care workers, have volunteered to be in the video. It is important that the whole of the undressing is shown, the removal of each item of clothing being mimed.

One or two clips are viewed by the whole group, the 'audience' being trainee care workers watching the video or attending the lecture-demo as part of their training.

This role activity is not directly related to the event of the suicide but is an attempt to include a more formal role activity such as might be found in a Mantle of the Expert role drama. It is the drama activity most removed from a living through event. Metaxis was not aimed for but, interestingly, it was strongly in evidence in places.

6. Working in groups of five, one of the group is the person (ideally a female so she can be a mother in the following scene) who has dismissed herself from the retirement home and moved into the family holiday home, much to the dismay of her family. It is a simple cabin, and it is the start of a glorious summer. She has decided she will die there – she is dying of cancer – and is eating very little if anything. The group has to rehearse a family scene that takes place at a mealtime. The mother has done all the cooking and insists on serving the meal and waiting on everyone. The children have different attitudes to the mother's action in moving out of the home and they know she intends to die at the cabin: one is strongly against it and thinks the whole situation is ridiculous, but wants to avoid a row and get back to his or her own life; one supports the mother but does not want to admit it; one is simply upset; and one does not know what to think. None of them paid much attention to her when she was in the home. The mother insists on doing everything for the family. It is her last act of parental love but she is finding it really difficult. The group is to rehearse the key moment of the meal, centring on an action.

This activity provides the opportunity to see what mode of involvement is employed in a presentation, using Bolton's (2010c: 40) definition of the term rather than calling it a performance. Also the audience can assess their own mode of involvement. It could be anticipated that the performers will be more in rational mode and the audience open to more feeling/emotion responses depending on the skill of the presenters. As it happened this was not always the case.

Commentary

My aim with this exercise was twofold: first to give the students the opportunity to force themselves to try to capture in retrospect the sorts of internal activities that were taking place, and second to test the presupposition that each of the above activities, being in a frame more distant from the first, would result in a more reasoned, reflective mode of enquiry. In fact the results confirmed my suspicion that a frame distance from an event can also be structured in such a way as to result in a 'living through' experience, at least in certain moments. They mainly became 'making' drama experiences. The original immersion in a story became key, and the story dimension became a strong reference point, so confirming the importance of storyline in the structures even for the out of role activity.

The collection of this sort of evidence cannot be regarded as research. The estimates of those involved in the activities were totally subjective. The forms were filled in privately and the students found it difficult to be sure what had happened to them. Nevertheless it proved revealing enough. One of the interesting results was that none of the activities resulted in a figure in only one or two columns. In each mode of involvement there were results for each category, even if some of them only rated a one. There tended to be a centre of gravity but this differed from student to student. This was partly because I had separated emotion from feeling. This enabled them to record, for example, that a high level of emotion had been experienced at a certain moment while being in what was mainly a rational thought mode (for example in the planning exercise).

In **Number 1,** the retirement home, some responses were at the high end of the emotion range. In fact, in one or two cases, the drama role situation became too much and the participant had to drop out or leave the room. (I had warned them in advance that if any of them found the experience too direct they should just quietly drop out.) This is when raw emotion takes over from the 'as if' emotion described by Bolton (2010a: 130–1) which, although also real emotion rather than simulated emotion, is tempered by the student's knowledge that it is not actually taking place. When something in the drama triggers a real memory, such as the participant remembering her own mother's time in a retirement home when she did not visit enough, then this can take over from the 'fictional' situation. This approach to emotion is dealt with more fully in Bolton (1986).

In **Number 2,** the pairs activity of collecting the belongings of the dead person (in reality their own belongings), the range of results was wide, from high levels of emotion to thinking feelingly as well as rational thought. This raises interesting questions about the responsibilities that alone belong to the 'actor' and this area became apparent in several of the improvisations, but more on this below.

In **Number 3,** the committee of enquiry, it might have been anticipated that the two carers under scrutiny would be the ones with high levels of emotion and feeling, but there were also high levels from the committee members. This was because TiR was able to open up the tensions between what should be a human response to the promise to dispose of the belongings and what should be the 'proper' institutional response. This was brought about by highlighting the official approach, the respectable approach, and this evoked a very mixed response from the students on the committee. Tempers flared and had to be kept under control because of the social situation in the drama: they simmered under the surface, occasionally breaking out. The carers sometimes lied and got themselves deeper and deeper into a mess.

Others brazened it out and told the truth, which brought down on them the wrath of some members of the committee.

In **Number 4,** the out of role activity, it might have been expected that the response would be rational, but there was also emotion, though not really to do with the experience of the situation. For example, joy might be experienced, along with the delight of being able to design an Elysium for the living and push aside the cares of the world. This highlights the need for the feelings, thoughts and emotions to be appropriate to the drama situation. This activity was included for comparison but also to provide a relief from the situation before continuing.

In **Number 5,** the demonstration, it might be anticipated that the responses would be at their most formal, with the demonstrators and the audience mainly in rational or thinking feelingly modes. The lecture demonstrations were carefully and responsibly prepared, but in many cases the results horrified the trainee care workers, as the reality of the indignity of old age began to be revealed in a way that had been hidden from them when they were rehearsing, i.e. when they had been focusing with rational thought. Also, several of the carers who were doing the demonstrating had this same shocked reaction. As one of them said, 'I suddenly asked myself: What on earth was I doing?' It was as though there had not been time to 'feel' the situation while they were rehearsing it.

In **Number 6,** although it is taken out of the home, it still closely relates to what has gone before and the participants drew strongly on the previous experiences. The presentations produced similar responses to those recorded in Number 5, probably because the presentation mode is not the same as the performance mode. There is often little time to rehearse; there may only have been time for a walk through before the sharing so the 'performance' has a 'living through' dimension to it which would disappear after many rehearsals and performances. For example, in one of the scenes the mother, quietly exasperated at the bickering of her children and their use of mobile phones, went to the window, opened it wide to let in the beautiful summer day and breathed in the perfume of the flowers in full bloom. She reported afterward that she felt exhilarated and just wanted to embrace the sky and disappear into it and leave behind forever the failure of a family she had 'nurtured'. She said that she understood for the first time why some people commit suicide.

The point I am pursuing in this section is that although the activities could broadly be seen as frame distanced, they are constructed around a loose narrative thread that holds together the possibility of structuring drama with the drama components in place. For example, in Number 3, the committee could be seen as 'authority' and the care workers as 'guide'. If, however, the 'authority' role had been set up as a committee whose role was to *read* the evidence, this might have been done in mainly rational thought mode. I argue that it all depends on the mode of involvement put into place and having the intention to 'make' drama. In this way frame and mode of involvement are always interrelated.

Protection into role and the 'second dimension'

A key dimension of any process drama is how the students are helped into the role. An actor in the theatre will likely have his or her own techniques for building a character, which will involve studying the play with a director and the other actors and spending a long time finding the connection between herself and the role. Often this can involve following Stanislavskian techniques, much to the detriment of the play, as I argue later. In process drama, entering role often has to be comparatively swift. It involves finding a connection with the role, not building a character. There are ways of aiding this process.

What will not work is expecting the participants to just 'be' in role. This is easily demonstrated by asking the student group to stand up and 'be' pirates. If they are willing students they will stand up and you will get people stomping around on a wooden leg with a parrot on a shoulder and the 'pirates' will be making each other walk the plank. Without preparation and help it is inevitable that the students will fall back onto empty clichés and stereotypical role types and feel embarrassed into the bargain. The further away from the actual life experience of the participants the more difficult it is to find a connection. Here one of the most useful and neglected areas of theory comes to the rescue. This is Bolton's notion of finding the second dimension of role, which was originally a set of notes for a weekend teachers' course in 1972. I know of only one place where this is published in full (Bolton, 1986: 40–1), with further elaboration in *Towards a Theory of Drama in Education* (Bolton, 1979: 57–60), although Bolton never seems to refer to it again as the second dimension. I draw attention to it in my introduction to his *Essential Writings* (Davis, 2010: xvi–xvii).

If we go back to the pirate example, another route to finding a connection with such a distant role could be the following steps. Again I describe the process schematically.

1. Explain that pirates were generally people who had put themselves outside the law. They were outlaws. In those times laws were harsh. A poverty-stricken person could be hanged for stealing a loaf of bread. Ask the students

to decide what they have done that would mean they would hang if caught. To escape punishment they have run away from home and put themselves outside the law. They have decided to join a pirate ship.

2. Ask them to imagine they are in a place like Bristol docks. It would be bustling with life: goods being loaded and unloaded; provisions being brought to the ships; carts trundling past. The problem is how to find which ship is a pirate ship. You cannot just ask someone. The participants need to find a place where they can see everyone and not stand out. They are asked to take up their places in the drama room. They tend to find a place with their backs to a wall.

3. They notice another young person standing around. They are to make eye contact and when they feel ready one of the two is to go to the other and see if s/he can find out as much as possible about the other and about the ships in the port while giving away as little as possible.

This has brought into play a second dimension of role. The first dimension is outlaw/pirate; the second is a wary person; someone who has to have eyes in the back of his head. You could find a way in through many second dimensions: home-sick young pirate; even love-sick pirate!

The second dimension needs to have four qualities:

a) it needs to be a quality of role that the child can relate to, one that belongs to his life experience

b) it needs to be a possible dimension of the role in question

c) it needs to bring the whole class together (presuming the whole class is entering the same role)

d) it needs to help the drama move forward.

It is not possible to just *be* firefighters but it is possible to find a way into being 'inexperienced' firefighters new to the job. Doctors can be 'empathetic' doctors; nurses can be 'patient' nurses; space travellers can be 'calm (in a crisis)'.

Another aid to protecting into role can be taken from Heathcote's 'Signs and Portents' (1984b). Here she is writing for TiE teams and pointing out that whereas the actors/teachers are paid to be stared at, the young people are not and need protecting. She suggests that anything they can focus on outside of themselves will make an 'other' and take the pressure away from the immediacy of stepping into role. It needs to be interactive. That is to say the activity presented must not be completed but offered incomplete. The activity of working on the 'other' works back onto the participants and edges them towards the role. Below are some examples I have used. They illustrate ways of using the scant resources the classroom drama teacher has to hand.

Security guards[2]

The students will probably have in mind: having power; having guns; getting into fights with criminals and so on. To avoid this, the teacher could give them an 'other' to focus on. Blackboards and whiteboards are invaluable here.

The teacher could pose a problem to the group out of role. Suppose a bank needs to put in place a security system. What sort of proposals/plans might a security firm put forward?

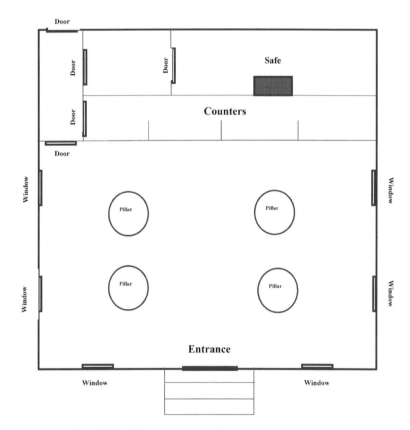

Figure 4.4: Plan of a bank

It is a bank that has taken over a rather grand old building with an imposing front, high ceilings, tall windows, wide steps leading up to the front door and four large pillars in the central hall. Here the teacher could draw the outline of the bank on the board. It would not need to be as detailed as the plan in Figure 4.4. The detail has been included here to make the idea clearer.

The class can then be asked what sort of suggestions a security firm might make if they were bidding for the contract, bearing in mind the budget has to be competitive. Students can come out and mark in and argue for their suggestions. A student might suggest security cameras in various places, for example. It is likely this will provoke discussion and argument about the best places to site them and how far they will scan. How can every part of the bank be covered with the least number of cameras? Whenever I have used this sort of example the discussion has grown and at some point on every occasion one of the participants says '*we* should ...' whereas I have been using the third person throughout. Teacher can now note those who are coming into role without them even realizing it and those who are still outside. At a certain point the teacher can slip into the first person and become TiR. A possible second dimension here is *vigilant* security guards.

Oil-rig workers

Here again board work is useful. The teacher can just draw the following outline on the board and simply write in 'Safety regulations – to be obeyed at all times'. The students will offer suggestions and these can be put to the class and written in. I have put a few that might come up in Figure 4.5.

Safety Regulations
(to be obeyed at all times)

1 Wear hard hats at all times

2 No running on external decking

3 No smoking except in designated areas

4 Only rubber-soled boots permitted

5 etc ...

Figure 4.5: Suggested safety regulations

As the rules are invented it becomes clearer and closer to the students what life is like on board an oil rig. There can be storms and slippery surfaces. There is a constant risk of explosions and fire and so on. The second dimension coming into play is to do with being *careful, alert to danger* oil-rig workers. Again, the students have an 'other' to focus on.

Black people in the Deep South of the USA

This is an example of a very difficult role if, for example, the participants are almost all white.

Teacher starts with a narration. S/he tells the real story of a black boy of about 12 whose older sister was the nanny for a white family and looked after two small children. One of these was a little girl with long blond curls. This little girl had grown to like the boy. They often met when his sister was taking the children out for a walk. One day the little girl saw the boy coming towards her and ran to him. He went down on his knees and opened his arms to welcome her and she flew into them. A passing white man was so disgusted that he informed the sheriff, who arrested the boy. He was charged with sexual assault, found guilty and sent to a penitentiary.

This is a first 'other' for the students to focus on. Good narratives always focus the attention. Then the class is invited to make a still image of members of the black community just outside the local store on a Sunday when they are not at work. The store has a large wooden veranda at the front. Students are invited to come out one by one and take up a still image. For example, one comes out and says 'I am a girl skipping while waiting for my mother to come out of the store'. Another child decides to join her. We get an elderly man smoking a pipe, two women chatting and so on. They make the whole composite picture and then half stay frozen while the other half looks at the image and then they swap over. They are asked to make another image showing the people of the community seeing the man who went to the police pass by. Again, each half sees the image made by the other half.

They have been protected by the story and then by the still image, which requires no speech. They are likely to have made a step towards being able to take on the role in question. Second dimensions that appeared when I tried this exercise ranged from *contemptuous/indignant* to *fearful* members of the community.

Norwegian teachers under the German occupation in the Second World War

I was given this role by a group of Norwegian teachers who wanted to set the drama during these troubled times. Luckily I had visited the museum in Oslo dedicated to what happened to education under the Occupation. One of the first things the Nazis did was to control the press and to control education. They changed the curriculum to make it pro-German. Every school classroom had to have a photograph of Hitler on display. Some of the first people to resist the Occupation were teachers who refused to comply. They were sent to terrible concentration camps in the far north.

The 'other' I thought of was to ask the students to imagine that the head of the local Gestapo was just about to make his first visit. They had had minimum notice. The head teacher was in a panic and had rushed out to the gate to wait for his arrival and had told the staff to get the seating in the hall ready for the meeting. I asked them how they thought those teachers would have arranged things. This left them out of role, discussing and moving the chairs around. They tried them all at the back of the hall with the guest table right at the other end. This looked too provocative. They decided to do without chairs and put the men at the front and then decided this looked too confrontational. And so it went on and, as usually happens, the language subtly changed from 'they would do this' to 'we should do this' and they were on their way to being protected into role. The second dimension that appeared was *defiant* teachers.

Pop stars

This is a role with the same potential as pirates to move straight into cliché. For this one I initiated a series of steps. I gave the students the situation that they were a band that had become very popular locally and had sent a demo disc to a promoter. They had received an invitation to go to the Sony headquarters to sign a contract. This was the pretext. They decided what sort of music it was and the class took on the shadow role of being in corporate role as the group (they were all members of the group even though there would have been fewer people in actuality). The shadow role foreshadows the actual role they will bring fully to life later. They were invited to make up the name of the group. (All play for class so far!) Then they had to choose the person to go to do the negotiating. They chose a girl who they decided was the lead singer. I asked her to come to the front and the rest of the group modelled her. That is, they decided what she should wear, how she should do her hair and her make-up, what her body language should be like, and so on. (More play for class and a good time had by all!) When she was ready I set up the office and told them I would be the person from Sony. I asked one of the class to take on the role of my personal assistant. The singer arrived and I kept her waiting outside my office and while I had my back to her made several phone calls on my mobile. When I finally sent for her I pushed the contract across the desk and, in order to unsettle her, asked her if that was how she normally dressed or if it was a stage image (very unkind!). I told her we were offering them a contract; we would have complete control over image, style of dress, the music they sang, where they did gigs, what records they made and so on. And we would be taking 70 per cent of the earnings in the first year. This could be renegotiated if the contract was renewed. It was a take it or leave it situation. After trying to negotiate, with me refusing to budge, she finally signed the contract just as I was about to withdraw it completely. When she went back to the group there was mayhem. Suddenly the students had taken a step closer to being real pop stars. The initial second dimension was *self-confident* pop stars but this later took on a dimension of being *nonplussed*. It needed the first to lead into the second.

Here I have only indicated an initial step towards role by starting to work with them out of role and providing an 'other' to focus on until this works back on them and enables them to find an authentic voice. To quickly illustrate how these can be built into a sequence we could take the oil-rig workers example. After drawing up the safety rules they could be asked to model one of the workers who has just finished onshore training stepping onto the deck from the helicopter that has flown him or her out to the rig. The helicopter blades are whirring overhead, the figure stooping, maybe looking up and clutching a backpack. When they are satisfied with the image they could be asked to assemble in the briefing room. They are now in role as 'rookies'. They are asked to take up a still image waiting for the briefing officer (TiR). The officer starts to tell them about life on board and not to fall into the trap that many rookies fall into – that of trying to tell the experienced hands how to do their job. 'Don't start telling them that what they are doing is breaking the rules. Those people who have been teaching you on shore don't live in the real world. Here we have targets to meet' and so on. It is a provocation and an invitation to speak for the first time, which would be difficult to do so it is no problem if no one dares to speak out. But when they are on their own it is likely to be a different story, especially if we are heading for disaster because we are cutting too many corners.

To recapitulate. A range of 'others' have been used: various forms of board work comprising lists and plans (but many others can be invented); narration; still images; modelling; arranging objects; and TiR itself. This is only a sample and others could be added. These start with the students out of role having something other than themselves to focus on. The activity works towards finding a second dimension of role, which provides a means of entering that role in an authentic way.

Role-playing

The final area to focus on is the one area for which the students have to take individual responsibility once the teacher has protected them into role. Just as the actor is a creative artist so is the role-player in process drama. There is a dimension to this sort of role-play that is to do with reading what I call the psychological present of the situation. Returning to the example of the father going into the stable to persuade his daughter to come into the house to take up her rightful place, there is that moment of apprehension when he stops at the door to take in the scene. The *actual* psychological moment he experiences will influence how he proceeds. If he senses a stiff, unrelenting posture he might take a conciliatory tack, speaking kindly and gently. Or if he sees an image of someone conjuring up her courage to do what she is doing, he perceives what might be a weakness somewhere. He decides to play the dead mother card. His first words are gentle 'You must miss your mother, don't you?' This is something not learned quickly; some will have it intuitively, others can begin to learn it.

Along with this reading of the situation moment to moment (which also applies to the teacher in role) the student is making decisions about the pacing of the interaction; the timbre, pitch, and loudness or softness of the voice; how to move in the space; what objects can be brought into play; when or if to touch another person and so on. None of this can be fed in from the teacher in a 'living through' situation. The greater the level of experience and the greater the conscious understanding of the art form the more the student should have to draw on. This is the 'I am making it happen' but the 'It is happening to me' never completely takes over. There is always *metaxis* present.

Along with the above the student needs to play her objective for all it is worth.

'Making' drama: A joint project

As mentioned previously, I do see the teacher and students working together to 'make' drama, sharing responsibilities. The aim would be, as progression in the drama syllabus occurs, for the student to gain greater understanding of the process, working towards greater command of the art form. I am sure the actor in the theatre cannot work without the director as interpreter of the author, but whether or not the student can ever 'make' drama independently of the teacher remains an open question for me. A division of labour in making drama might look like the following:

Areas of Responsibility
Joint teacher/student responsibility
• The nature of the art form • Components of the art form • Meaning making
Teacher prime responsibility
• Five layers of meaning • Using hidden information • Relevance and significance • Secondary symbolism and the angle of connection • Sequencing and internal coherence • Frame distance • Modes of involvement
Teacher responsibility moving to joint responsibility
• Protection into role
Sole student responsibility
• Role-playing

Conclusion

This is a basic account of key dimensions of 'making' drama. I have had to leave out other important areas such as, teacher in role; the nature and role of emotion in process drama; semiotics; progression and so on. There is not space here to cover all these important elements and skill areas. My aim is to introduce just enough to begin to explore how they might be developed from a Bondian perspective.

Notes

[1] Peter Brook would say this is theatre. I do not agree. If that were the case then, for example, every time we watched someone in an empty room it would be theatre.

[2] This example is adapted from one Heathcote worked on with my student group.

Chapter 5

A process drama

This outline of a longer process drama illustrates the sort of 'making' drama and 'being' in role I advocate above.

Over the last few years my work has been with adult teachers on in-service courses. I have worked the following drama with teachers, predominantly women and a few men, in Greece, Turkey and Palestine. Many were parents, so they were immediately drawn to the central concerns of the problems of disciplining children and child abuse. This influenced my choice of material and how the drama was structured, but not the content. It would work equally well for students aged 15 plus, but the structure and the way they were introduced to the material and engaged with the role would need to be adapted to suit their interests.

I have chosen to use a drama that I have tried and tested comparatively recently. If actually working with teenagers I am supposing that the topic has come up through a previous drama done or it has sprung from an interest in topical events. I am also supposing that the class is not necessarily very experienced in drama. This lack of experience was true of the teachers I worked with, some of whom had not done drama before. The less experience in drama the class has, the more structuring by the teacher there needs to be. A teacher could work in a much more open-ended way with classes highly experienced in drama.

It is a drama about the family, the state, law and justice. The drama is set a few years in the future and explores a fictitious country attempting to get rid of child abuse and violence against young children by making it illegal. This is not told to the participants at the start of the drama, but comes up as the structure proceeds. I have set out the structure in detail as a series of numbered tasks with a description of the activity and teacher thinking in italics immediately following. I have embedded the several handouts in the text to make for easier reading.

Process drama on child abuse

Note: In the following structure the teacher participants are referred to as students to make it more classroom friendly and the session leader is referred to as the teacher for the same reason. It can be completed in three or four hours, broken into several units or take longer if the teacher decides to spend more time on the middle set of improvisations.

1. The teacher makes a fresh contact with the class and then reminds them of the area of interest that arose in a previous session and introduces the idea of a drama on child abuse, asking if they are willing to give it a try. If it does not appeal after giving it a good try then it will be necessary to negotiate another way forward or another drama.

It is useful to have a contact/contract stage. This enables the teacher to read the mood and readiness for drama. The contact stage cannot be prepared in advance but is an intuitive initiative on the part of the teacher. If the class is unusually subdued, for example, the teacher might start with, 'You seem a bit down today?' Someone might answer 'We have just been told off' and so on. This enables fresh and real contact to be made between teacher and class. It is useful to bear in mind that, in an important sense, the teacher has never met that class before: that is to recognize that they are different in some small or large way even since the previous week. The contract stage needs to be a genuine one. My own approach would always be to honour their response. If they rejected the idea of the drama offered I would accept it and we would be off somewhere else. We can always come back to child abuse later. The contract might be offered as 'Last week you got interested in child abuse so I have come up with an idea of a drama exploring that topic. Are you OK with giving it a go?' If the answer is a yes, then you have some sort of contract and the class has made a step towards owning the drama.

2. To start to find a way into the themes of the drama the students are invited to find a partner, asking them to make mixed-gender pairings where possible. Mixed-gender interactions are more likely to become effective quickly. They are asked to make a still image of mother/child love. They need to decide on the age of the child.

Working in mixed-gender pairings is not an absolute. Cross-gender role-playing may be very useful but be uncomfortable for students new to drama and may take time to get used to. I have chosen mother/child as the group is made up predominantly of women so there will always be enough mothers and the child can be boy or girl. Again my decision was made in the cultural circumstances where the mother is often the primary carer even if both parents are working. It could also just be parent and child.

This also serves as an early diagnostic stage when the teacher can observe how they set about the task and read the group's readiness for work, their social health, and, most importantly, what they understand by parental love. Some pairs might depict brushing a daughter's hair, reading the child a story etc. – whatever they think demonstrates 'love'.

3. When they have had time to prepare, one half shows the other half their depictions, and those watching say what they see, not what they think is happening. Then some interpretations of the actions could be offered. After this the other half does the same.

It is important, for me at least, at this stage to start with what they see. The teacher can illustrate the difference between interpretation and actually looking closely at something. The students will tend to rush to meaning, which is their personal interpretation of the action. When held to what they see, for example, 'I see a mother kneeling behind her daughter with a brush in one hand and hair in the other, leaning round to look at the result from the front' then it is possible later to move to possible readings of meanings: 'The mother seems to be more interested in her child's appearance than getting tangles out of the hair.' Whether to see all the pairs' still images or only two or three from each half of the group depends on a number of factors. There is the question of the time available, and then again the class may need to go slowly as they are feeling their way and the teacher might decide to give them all due respect. This might be negotiated differently in mid-stream if the class seems to have had enough. There are no rules for this sort of interaction. It is a question of teacher always being in the moment.

There is then a chance to share their thinking about parental love.

4. Giving them plenty of time, each pair will plan a moment of violence from the mother to the child. Each pair will decide what the child has done (or not done) to cause the mother to behave like that and then work out and rehearse how to show a slow motion representation of the action.

The word 'violence' is inserted deliberately. It might seem an extreme descriptor but any physical reprimand will become a 'violent' act later in the drama. It also tends to imply it is physical, as violence could also be verbal and this would not work in the next step.

5. The pairs get into a circle and pair by pair they show their slow motion moment of violence. I ask 'Why are you doing that?' and the mother has to reply 'Because ...' and gives the agreed reason of that pair. What we see might be a range of examples, from a mother giving a child a slap in a supermarket for knocking some products over, to shaking a child because s/he has been rude to the mother.

6. This leads into an open discussion about child abuse and violence. For example: Were all these examples of violence? Was the chastisement

necessary? Is it a form of bullying? Is any form of punishment bad for a child? And so on.

Note that there are no right or wrong answers. The particular questions cannot all be worked out in advance. The questions are based on a reading of the group's depicted actions. Also, the sequence of activities in a drama structure needs to be internally coherent for the students. There are not sudden jumps in logic that would jar with what is going on in the students' heads. Each step in the structure needs to be internally coherent and prepare for the next activity. This is not the equivalent of a series of conventions. This process is developing the basis for a story.

7. The teacher introduces the fact that these concerns have been discussed at the highest level in the United Nations General Assembly and hands out photocopies of the extract from the UN Rights of the Child. The teacher reads it out and they discuss it. Do they agree with it or not? (See copy of handout below.)

Convention on the Rights of the Child

Adopted and opened for signature, ratification and accession by United Nations General Assembly resolution 44/25 of 20 November 1989

Article 19

1. States Parties shall take all appropriate legislative, administrative, social and educational measures to protect the child from all forms of physical or mental violence, injury or abuse, neglect or negligent treatment, maltreatment or exploitation, including sexual abuse, while in the care of parent(s), legal guardian(s) or any other person who has the care of the child.

2. Such protective measures should, as appropriate, include effective procedures for the establishment of social programmes to provide necessary support for the child and for those who have the care of the child, as well as for other forms of prevention and for identification, reporting, referral, investigation, treatment and follow-up of instances of child maltreatment described heretofore, and, as appropriate, for judicial involvement.

The teacher invites comment, asking for example, how it relates to the moments of violence we saw earlier.

8. The class is asked if they would be willing to take on the role of trainee members of a unit of special child protection officers in a fictitious country some years in the future. This country has lagged behind the Conventions on the Rights of the Child and now intends to adopt them and stamp out child abuse of any sort.

Again, there is a contract stage here when they are asked if they are willing to take on the role of trainees. It is important that they are trainees. This means that they do not have to 'know the ropes' but are learning their role. Also important is that they are clear that the drama is set in a fictitious country and in the future. This enables resonance with the present but the freedom to invent without the constraint of bringing contemporary social features into play. Presuming teacher gets a 'yes' then the drama moves to a new stage with the next section, where they are starting to build their role, step by step. If they say 'no' then the teacher has to address that. There will be no worthwhile drama with a class not motivated or interested in the subject matter.

Note that the teacher deliberately uses a phrase like 'stamping' out child abuse to begin to lay this rather ambiguous approach to the problem: we will use violent means to end violence, but, of course, this is not made explicit at this stage.

9. The teacher draws their attention to a new law that the country in question has just passed to provide the legal basis for the 'fight' against child abuse.

When appropriate the teacher adopts a shadow role approach from here on. That is the teacher hints at the role s/he will take later in the drama by slightly increasing the tone of authority, for example, or using certain phrases such as 'child abuse must be eradicated' or 'we have to stamp it out' or, as above, the 'fight' against child abuse, and so on, but avoiding being too crude about this.

The central influence on the TiR is the image of the Prince striding in in Romeo and Juliet *to solve the social problems facing the young people and directly feeding in to the tragic ending by banishing Romeo; or more accurately, Creon, determined that social mores and laws should be maintained, ignoring the human imperative, represented by Antigone, staring him in the face.*

The new law 4 below is handed out to each member of the class but the teacher does not invite discussion about it. The teacher reads it out and it is presented as a matter of fact.

On 19 October 2016, Parliament passed Law 3500/2016 on the Combating of Intra-family Violence, under which corporal punishment of children within the family is prohibited.

Article 4 of the new law states: 'Physical violence against children as a disciplinary measure in the context of their upbringing brings the consequences of Article 1532 of the Civil Code.'

Article 1532 of the Civil Code provides for various consequences for abuse of parental authority, the most serious being the removal of parental authority by the courts.

This new law, which comes into force on 1 January 2017, will now form the basis of a public education campaign to be launched by the Families Network aimed at raising awareness of the need to end the use of corporal punishment of children.

The teacher reading it out brings another opportunity for the teacher's shadow role, foreshadowing the TiR as training officer, which is explained later.

10. Teacher explains that if neighbours or teachers or anyone (it can be anonymous) reports a suspicion of child abuse in the home then special police implement surveillance of the home in question. Surveillance of all types might be used: video, bugging devices, wiretapping, photography and so on. Their role as child protection officers will be to receive the reports of this surveillance and they will have the power and the duty to recommend the child be taken into care and the adults in question charged under the above act. These officers will collect the child and place him or her in care. Teacher makes it clear that they are not full police officers but they will have powers of arrest – they are a subdivision of the police and are still undergoing training.

11. Teacher hands out an application form for the job and asks the class to imagine that this was the form they filled in when they applied for the job. They fill it in as they did then. (See below.)

The filling in of the form begins a liminal stage for the participants where they are between being out of role and immersed in the role. (See Turner, 1982 for a full discussion of liminal and liminoid activities. For example in some cultures it is the state during the rite of passage between childhood and adulthood. Liminal has become used in a much looser way to mean betwixt and between and I use it in this more general sense. It differs from metaxis, which I see as fully in role where the actual and the fictional exist together at the same time.) This liminal stage lasts for quite a while. I signal later the first time they are actually asked to bring the role into physical action. The filling in of the form is a classic Heathcote device to begin the process of protecting into role and moves them step by step from out of role into role.

APPLICATION FORM THREE FOR SPECIAL CHILD PROTECTION OFFICERS (SUBSECTION OF POLICE FORCE)

NAME

AGE

MARITAL STATUS

Married/Divorced/Single (please delete the ones that do not apply)

NUMBER OF DEPENDENTS (if applicable)

EDUCATION/QUALIFICATIONS

....

....

....

....

RELEVANT EXPERIENCE (continue overleaf if necessary)

[Larger space here in original]

REASONS FOR WANTING TO JOIN THE CHILD PROTECTION UNIT (continue overleaf if necessary)

[Larger space here in original]

EXPERIENCE WITH CHILDREN/YOUNG PEOPLE (continue overleaf if necessary)

[Larger space here in original]

Notice that it is form three. This implies a bureaucracy at work. They have had to fill in many forms and it has been a multistage application process.

12. Teacher gathers in the application forms and narrates that this was part of a lengthy selection process in which they were all successful. She then asks them to set up their workspace – they are still at the training stage but this will be their office from which eventually they will work. They work in teams and the training course simulates the real work they will do. They are asked to divide into teams of four or five, depending on the size of the class, and then, as a team, to mark out their team workspace with masking tape

and draw on paper where shared equipment is and where their individual work items are kept.

As a team, they tape out their workspace, for example where their desks are, or they may choose shared desks and just mark out their workspace, then draw on paper a PHONE TO SHARE and a FAX MACHINE TO SHARE, and mark out the area of their team NOTICEBOARD on a nearby wall.

Individually, they draw a COMPUTER EACH, a FILING CABINET EACH and whatever they think they would have in their individual workspace.

Note they are not yet in role but building the role. They have not been asked to speak or act in role yet.

They can also add anything else they care to think of such as pooled car keys, coats and bags, and so on.

Ideally they will need a chair each and a wall space (the wall space nearby for a noticeboard for each team but no more).

They also create their individual workspace with their name (drama name or actual name) displayed and computer and keyboard plus any personal objects such as family photographs.

The chance to make a family photograph or similar personal object brings the personal into the social. Up to this point they have been creating a work environment. But people often take something of their personal lives into their workspaces. It is a reminder of their 'real' life. This also, without making it explicit, requires them to draw on what they have written on their forms and enables them to continue particularizing what would otherwise be a very general role.

13. Each team creates their team noticeboard. Teacher asks what sort of things might be on the noticeboard. Then each person creates one of each of the following: an official, a personal and an office management item. Each team is given a copy of the new government law and the UN Conventions on the Rights of the Child to add to the noticeboard.

This continues the process of edging into role and brings a range of frames to bear: international, national, management and personal. The personal is key to what comes later.

14. Teams are given an opportunity to browse each other's noticeboards.

15. Students are asked to pair with another from the same team (or a three if in a group of five) and, over tea or coffee, they are asked to share one personal thing each. Teacher might illustrate by telling them something one of their children did the night before, or that happened in the car park or while shopping and so on. An option in setting this up is to ask them to make

a still image of the moment just before they begin to share and then to start them all off together.

This is the first time they have been asked to bring the role to life. It provides another opportunity for the teacher to assess how ready they are to begin role-playing. Timing when to signal the end of an improvisation that the whole class is creating in pairs or groups is always a difficult one to judge. I tend to warn a class that I will stop them when most seem ready to do so but also warn them that some may feel they would like to have had longer. On the other hand those who 'run out of steam' too soon are encouraged just to sit quietly and look around them at others or talk quietly about what they have just done.

16. Teacher warns them that at a signal from the teacher they will all be busy, as part of their training session, working on one of the cases just reported to them, which they will need to invent for themselves. All are given time to invent a case, then what they will be doing: for example, writing a report; catching up on some filing; faxing; emailing; phoning; asking a colleague for something or asking their opinion. If needed, have paper and pens ready.

If what has gone before has worked they should now feel comfortable with the role they are creating. If they choose to talk to another in the team this should happen easily, but they can be doing something on their own if that feels more comfortable.

17. Each Child Support Officer (CSO), staying in role, is asked to invent memories stirred up by the work – one thing experienced as a child and one done as an adult, involving corporal punishment or neglect or abuse – and write about this as a short entry in a diary, for example in the form of a poem or a confession.

Although they are not interacting, the staying in role is important in order to invent that memory in the role of the CSO they are creating. This brings the personal into the social in the role situation, but also they will most likely be drawing on their own experiences as a child and adult and this is part of the process of metaxis. It would be useful to observe if objects begin to appear as these might be useful to draw on later. The writing or drawings are kept personal and not shared with the group.

18. The teacher in role (TiR) then introduces him or herself to the whole class as shadow TiR, by saying, for example, 'I will be your unit in-service trainer' and addresses them in role, saying such things as 'child abuse is still happening in our country even though we have new laws – we needed this crusade against child violence and we have got it – we have set up these

sorts of units and been very successful – we have had many, many successful prosecutions – now here in this city the crusade has got going – when a report comes in a surveillance team goes out to collect the evidence – we use recording equipment, photos etc. but need to set ourselves some guidelines', and so on.

I have called it a shadow role as this is the first time they have all been in role together and the teacher needs to feel her way. By pitching the TiR on the cusp of being fully in role and almost totally there enables the reading of group readiness to continue to be assessed and allows them the comfort of also being on the cusp of being fully in role. It is important that words like 'crusade' are beginning to enter the vocabulary. The TiR is a keen advocate of the law and verges on being a closet zealot disguised as a reformer. These are only guidance notes to what the teacher in role needs to cover. Also worth noting is that the class is in listening/interactive mode, not needing to initiate anything unless anyone wants to, so they are still protected. It is important that they remain in role until the end of the drama.

19. TiR asks the teams to each make three short scenes to go in a training video, depicting scenes of potential child maltreatment in order to find the line between what is acceptable punishment of children and what is not: a) acceptable (would not need to report to higher authority for action); b) unacceptable (would have to report); c) on the borderline (difficult to know how to respond). The team, staying in role, needs to come to an agreement about each one as part of their training. Each scene should be no more than a few minutes long and they are asked to start immediately on their feet rather than planning them.

It is important to limit the time to show and prepare. This can be done in role by the training officer. They are now preparing drama within a drama. This is the turning point in the drama as they are talking and planning together as a team. The role-play should be comfortable both in primary and secondary roles. Again the use of the word punishment is deliberate. It is not a word that sits comfortably with parenting but it fits the drama situation and it is surprising how many adults are happy with this term.

20. The whole class of CSOs watch each other's replays of the incidents. TiR asks the rest of the group 'What is happening here?' The trainees try to come to a whole unit consensus about which category is which.

It is useful to see all of the group scenes. There is usually much discussion here. This will take time. They can be in random order from each group, which means that the rest of the CSO unit do not know which one they are watching and the TiR deliberately asks what is happening. The training officer aims for consensus as they will need that in their work but it also forces the issues. This reminds them regularly of the work they are preparing for.

21. As a training exercise TiR gives each team an envelope containing a set of lines that has been cut up so each line is on a separate piece of paper. (These are shown below as if set out on an A4 sheet but they would be cut into individual lines and placed in an envelope, one envelope for each team.) The teams must try to make sense of and work out the order in which the lines were said and by whom. The lines are presented as an in-service training exercise but it is a real case and the fact that it is needs to be underlined. It is like work experience, dealing with an actual report of a problem with a real family in a real situation. Neighbours of an immigrant family have made complaints and police have had to instigate surveillance of the house (listening devices, cameras and so on). The transcription from audio recordings became muddled during translation but these are the words that were said and, by implication, the things done, although it is not clear exactly what happened or who said what. It is known that it is an immigrant family and there is a man and a mother and daughter, but it is not known whether the man is the father. Each team takes an envelope of these jumbled lines to try to decipher and make sense of the situation. Each team needs to decide if there is a case to prosecute and a child to be taken into protection.

Below are the lines that would be cut into single lines and put into envelopes so they are in a random order. The font would need to be large enough to be seen easily by the whole team.

BE QUIET FOR GOD'S SAKE

(SOUND OF BANGING)

I WON'T TELL YOU AGAIN

THAT'S NOT NOISY REALLY

IT IS FOR ME – SHUT HER UP OR I WILL

BE QUIET OR I'LL WALLOP YOU

FETCH MY DINNER

(SOUND OF CHILD SCREAMING)

WHY DID YOU HIT HER?

SHE DESERVED IT

YOU SHOULDN'T DO IT SO HARD

I'LL CLOSE YOUR MOUTH IN A MINUTE

HANG HER UP ON THE BACK OF THE DOOR – THAT'LL KEEP HER OUT OF THE WAY

NO – TIE HER TO HER CHAIR FOR A BIT – THEN WE CAN GET A BIT OF PEACE

(*Indistinct – sounds like*) WA ... FOOD

SHUT YOUR MOUTH

THERE THAT'S BETTER

CAN I HAVE SOMETHING TO EAT

(*Indistinct – sounds like*) ... UNGRY

PUT A GAG ROUND THAT MOUTH WILL YOU

(CHOKING SOUND)

LOOK – SHE'S SHIT HERSELF – ALL OVER THE CHAIR – SHE'S AN ANIMAL

22. TiR underlines that even though this exercise is part of their training, this is a genuine case and now they have to do something about it. TiR tells them that they will act on the majority view. It is the stage of their training when they begin to put their training into practice. They are instructed to open their envelopes, take out the phrases, which will by now be in random order, and grouping round their phrases, preferably around a small table, discuss the order that they think might be correct, identify who said what, and try to come to a decision about whether or not to recommend

prosecution, but allowing differences of opinion to remain. Each group can then share their order and thoughts with the other groups.

It is important that individuals are not pressurized into making a group consensus but encouraged to come to an independent judgement.

23. TiR has prepared in advance a large sheet of paper with two columns headed PROSECUTE and DO NOT PROSECUTE. This is placed on the wall and each trainee is asked to sign in the column where their decision lies. If the decision is for prosecution the child will be put into protection in a care home, and the parents will be arrested and charged. Each CSO has to sign one way or the other and a pen is placed on a chair at the front. They come out one at a time.

The encouragement of an independent judgement in the previous stage now comes to the fore. All have to sign one side or the other. Those who are not sure are likely to wait before they sign. The large sheet of paper makes it an open process and allows any one of them to move their signature to the other side if there is a change of mind. There should not be a long reflective process at this stage. In fact it is better if the signing is done in silence. They will go with their immediate feelings about the case. The signing process gives time to think and time for individual reflection, which is different to talking it through, where thinking is modified by other opinions in the group. Each time it has been tried out a minority has gone against prosecution while the majority has gone for prosecution.

24. What happens next depends on who signed in which column. TiR explains that those who signed for prosecution are to work in groups (their original teams where possible, and amalgamating teams where some have decided against prosecution) and plan to go and collect the child and take her into care. Those who did not sign for prosecution will take on the role of the child and adults in question: three taking the roles and any others acting as advisers to them.

Working in groups, those who signed to collect the child plan precisely how they would take the child into custody: would they take a toy, a book, sweets, use cuddles or just be formal and announce the legal decision that had been made? They would need to decide how old they thought the child was. They are asked to plan and try it out in their groups, working separately from other groups.

Out of role, the teacher works separately with those who did not sign for the child to be taken into protection, if possible out of sight of the others. They are asked by teacher, out of role, to make some sort of paper location or drawings indicating the environment they think the child was in. Creating a paper location is to draw indications of the living conditions or anything else that they think evokes the living conditions of the immigrant family. In practice, one group drew dirty dishes, peeling wallpaper and so on, and also a little romantic painting of what might once have been their idealized picture of their home in their own country. Teacher explains that the child to be collected has cerebral palsy and cannot talk clearly or sit on her own and is, in fact, strapped in a wheelchair. TiR demonstrates how the child might be to give a real feel to it – the child cannot control her hands properly, they fly about, her head shakes, she makes incoherent noises as though she is trying to form words. They try out their roles and invent a still image they will make the moment when the knock comes on the door.

It is important that this scene is carefully prepared with the student playing the child having time to try it out without the class observing what is happening. This may curtail the trying out or they may be allowed outside the room to rehearse. The father is encouraged not to be stereotypically angry but much more likely to be afraid of authority (he might not have identity papers). The mother is encouraged to find her stance, which is likely to attempt to be protective of her child.

25. One of the prosecution groups volunteers to try out its idea for taking the child into custody and serving notice on the couple that they are to be prosecuted. As this is a real case, it was videoed as part of the training and the rest of the groups sit and watch as though watching the video as part of a training session. Remind them it is the actual situation not a simulation.

The family take up their still image when they hear the knock on the door signalling the arrival of the child protection officers. They then bring the event to life to see what happens. For example, only one of the adults may have some 'English', the child has soiled herself in fright and so on.

It is important to note the type of role-playing being developed here. The adults are being prepared for the role-play by building their situation. What will feed into this is how they have come to understand the situation of this immigrant 'family' and the problems they face. Their whole approach is that they will NOT BE ACTING but BEING in the role, i.e. they are and are not themselves in that role, both at the same time. The child is different. Here the teacher coaches the student playing the child as an actor, perhaps demonstrating how a child with cerebral palsy cannot control her head and arms so they wave about and in a moment of high tension she may make noises rather than speak. This prepares for a visceral impact on those watching rather than a verbal impact.

26. TiR needs to switch off the 'video' while the tension is still high. The CSOs, of course, have no idea that the child has cerebral palsy before they arrive. They do not have the means to take the child away. They do not know what they are going to do with her. And the parents will be prosecuted and so on.

One of the important skills of the drama teacher is to feel when to stop activities. Usually the rule of thumb is to stop them while they are in full flow and have not lost their impetus. It will all depend on how the CSOs have decided to proceed. They may have decided on a softly, softly approach or to be very distant and official with the adults at least. The important thing is for teacher to be sensitive to what is actually occurring.

27. The reflection on what has occurred can take several forms: staying in role, all the trainees back at the training course discuss with TiR what lessons can be learned from this exercise; out of role, reflecting on what took place; or teacher may just decide to leave it there for that session, the power of the moment staying with the students for internal reflection. In fact, it may work well to leave the reflection until later.

Discussing in role has the advantage of being trapped in the role and TiR can reinforce the official line. What becomes clear is that there are no easy answers. They are in the double bind of needing to protect children but questioning if this is the way to do it.

Final note: *This is all highly teacher-structured. As classes get better at drama and teacher more comfortable, then progressively there is room for student direction and suggestions from them, leading to their ability to structure, but for the learning dimension they are likely to need teacher involvement for a long time.*

Reflection

In the various discussions afterwards the questions they raised with each other were of this kind: Why did we think the law could solve huge social problems? What is the relationship between law and justice? Are we working in the same way in our daily work as teachers? Have we lost sight of the human? What is staring us in the face but goes unseen because of routinized structures? Something has to be done about child abuse, we can't just ignore it, but what needs to be done? And of course there were those who defended taking the child into custody and so on. They are the questions the teacher could prompt if the students are not at the level of asking questions of this sort.

Additional note

The central influence on those in role is the steady way we are 'institutionalized' or rather, through work routines, we begin to carry out the rules and ways of the institution where we are working so we may lose sight of what we are doing, just as we do in society and teachers do in schools. We come to accept the rules of the institution or the system and believe we are teaching children and running a just society or at least working for it. This is the thinking behind the long building into role. The TiR needs to use language like 'We have to get this campaign going' and 'There are not going to be any more children abused on my watch if I can help it' and so on, but it is important not to overdo or caricature it. The TiR needs to come across as a 'good' person, with all the dangers that implies. The centre of the drama raises the question of whether or not social problems can be resolved by laws: does law lead to justice? We are surrounded by new laws now and they are flowing out like water but is society more just?

The strongest response was from the Palestinian participants who, above all others, have daily experience of the injustice of the law. In considering their experience of the drama, two of the participants wrote the following:

> The drama about the child protection officers we feel is the most powerful one we've experienced. It had a long lasting effect on us – we talked and thought a lot about it and about our decision and its impact on the whole family and the child herself.

Then they commented separately:

> X (male): It was the first drama that created a huge conflict inside me – I felt I was two persons in one thinking about the conflict between law and humanity which rose up from the decision I had to make in the drama which was to save a child by the name of the law. Then I found myself in an encounter between the child who represents our helpless humanity and law in whose name a lot of human rights are violated. I found myself almost collapsed because of the big conflict I suffered and couldn't find lots of answers to its questions ... not sure what I am presenting – the law or the humanity. Was I with the torturer or the victim?
>
> The law is so important and it is not an absolute evil ...
>
> Y (female): I thought on the one hand as a mother and having a child and on the other as a child protection officer and in both roles thinking, how should I protect her?

Has anyone the right to decide for me or for her what is better for us? Could I refuse and stand face to face towards the law? Taking her could be helpful or painful to me and her – at the beginning of the drama I was thinking of protecting children and at the middle I was the one who must take a decision about it and when I signed taking the child and then seeing its case I felt so angry towards myself and blamed myself a lot because I had signed, and kept telling myself and the others 'I shouldn't have signed – I need another chance to change it.'

We can remember that the drama session dominated our minds and the members of the class talked together for more than that day. We all agreed that it was a very strong area we didn't experience before. We discussed how the law can be wrong and unjust or unfair. Many blamed themselves for signing.

The end of the drama was so surprising for us. We didn't expect it and we were shocked when we saw the girl.

We can remember also that all the members of the workshop talked about it and they even told it to the other students and teachers.

This is not meant to appear self-congratulatory. I merely wanted some evidence that it had worked. The main impetus for the participants to question their perspectives seems to have been, as was the intention, being faced with actually dealing with the whole problem of child abuse held in the moving image of the child and the adults – the child scarcely capable of speaking and in the fear of the moment only able to make noises and move her head and arms about uncontrollably. It was not through talking about it, but by being faced with it viscerally that reflection on it was stimulated.

Conclusion

This process drama illustrates some of the areas of theory covered previously. It places the participants both in their present actual world and a fictional future society. The *metaxis* effect is described by the first participant quoted above: 'I felt I was two persons in one, thinking about the conflict between law and humanity'. It aims to enable the students to 'make' a drama that is encouraging a certain mindset that they are free to reject (signing or not signing) and is then challenged in a mode of involvement that engages emotions, thoughts and feelings. There is a deliberately lengthy process of protecting into role with the intention, in a minor key, of imitating the way we tend to become taken over by ideology and a certain set of attitudes where we no longer continue questioning fundamental life values. The drama situation enables a check on what the participants are doing and how they are seeing and understanding the social world of which they are part. Each step in the sequence is internally coherent. The participants have counter-objectives in the key event of taking the child into custody and this holds the moment just long enough to begin to explore the reality of the situation they have brought into being. Levels of meaning are implicit in the event of attempting to take the child into custody, raising the question of whether or not this is how life should be. They are framed differently at different stages of the drama. For example, when trying to sort out the dialogue they are in a type of authority role; those who go to collect the child are in a sort of agent role, with those watching in a sort of critic role but all the time the teacher is aiming for them to be experiencing an event. Every drama will use the components differently and draw on what is needed to enable the students to succeed in bringing that drama to life.

Rather than analyse this example of process drama further, Part Three offers an analysis of this lesson from a Bondian perspective.

Part Three

3

Chapter 6

Towards a new theory of 'making' drama

Introduction

> I think the brain is essentially a computer and consciousness is like
> a computer program.
>
> (Stephen Hawking)

> What a piece of work is a man! how noble in reason!
> how infinite in faculty! in form and moving how
> express and admirable! in action how like an angel!
> in apprehension how like a god! the beauty of the
> world! the paragon of animals!
>
> (*Hamlet*, II, ii)

Of all the major European post-Second World War playwrights Edward
Bond has been a lone voice in consistently criticizing Brechtian theatre and
developing, in the writing of some fifty plays and in sustained theoretical
work, an alternative theory and practice. He categorizes Brechtian theatre
as aiming to 'create understanding through reason' (Bond, 2000: 11). But
what is wrong with reason? Surely we need a world of reason, a new Age
of Reason? I have spent many pages of this book criticizing the influence
of Brecht on DiE which has led to a reflective, distanced approach for role-
taking with reasoning very much to the fore. On the other hand I would
champion the Age of Reason, which was the title of a treatise by Thomas
Paine challenging institutionalized religion and which has become a term
pretty well synonymous with the European Enlightenment. The Radical
Enlightenment went further than the deistic writings of Paine, revolutionary
though they were, and provided a set of principles that formed the basis
of much modern progressive thought. These principles 'can be summed
up concisely as: democracy; racial and sexual equality; individual liberty
of lifestyle; full freedom of thought, expression, and the press; eradication

of religious authority from the legislative process and education; and full separation of church and state' (Israel, 2010: vii–viii).

The Enlightenment was an age of questioning and searching, stretching from the early 1600s to the early 1800s, shaking up thinking which had hardly changed since Aristotle. Shakespeare's *Hamlet* in 1601 could be said to open this age of questioning and individual responsibility. The Enlightenment involved figures such as Bacon, Hobbes, Newton and Descartes right through to Kant, alongside giants in the arts such as Goya and Beethoven.

France became the centre of the activity. Most people have heard of Voltaire and Rousseau, two of the Moderate Enlightenment thinkers, but the Radical Enlightenment thinkers were, in my opinion, far more important: d'Holbach, Diderot, d'Alembert, Helvétius and Condorcet among the leading figures, with Spinoza regarded as their founding father. As Hegel later acknowledged: 'to be a follower of Spinoza is the essential *commencement* of all philosophy' (Hegel, 1955: 257).

The courage of these thinkers should not be underestimated. Censorship was driven by state and church. Dubious publications were shredded and burned; the authors, if identified, jailed or exiled. This led to many of the dissident publications being smuggled abroad and printed there. The majority of the population was considered an ignorant mass on whose backs the aristocracy lived in luxury. Jails, the gallows and penal servitude were the order of the day. For example, 'In Holland hundreds of men were executed for the "crime" of homosexuality during a wave of fierce persecution in the 1730s' (Israel, 2010: 50). Any thought that the majority of the population could or should be educated, given a voice or even allowed to think anything other than official dogma was quickly ridiculed or worse. Yet, by the end of the eighteenth century Diderot and his co-authors were calling for the downtrodden of the world to rise against oppressors (99). These thoughts fed directly into the political movements of the French and American Revolutions even though many of the Enlightenment thinkers preferred the idea of a revolution of reason.

Spinoza was part of the exiled Jewish community in Amsterdam who had fled from the threat of persecution in Spain. He was 8 years old when Uriel da Costa, a member of Spinoza's community, decided to confess that he had been wrong in his writings so the two *cherems* (excommunications) that had been laid on him would be lifted. Da Costa had argued against the validity of the Talmud, argued against the immortality of the soul. The *cherem* ordered that he be:

> ostracised as a sick man, cursed by the Law of God; that no one, no matter what their rank, speak with him, whether they be man or woman, parent or stranger; that no one enter into the house he is occupying nor show him any favor, under the penalty of being included under the same *cherem*.
>
> (Nadler, 1999: 70)

Da Costa remained defiant and published a second book in the same vein. He was jailed, as the book was deemed as insulting to Christians as to Jews. All his books were burned and only one copy survived. He retaliated with an even more defiant book arguing that the Law of Moses was a human invention. A new *cherem* was passed against him and this time he chose to recant in order to have the ban lifted, probably because he wanted to marry. He was called before the synagogue, which was packed with men, women and children. He had to read out his recantation and was then stripped to the waist. Thirty-nine lashes were administered, after which he had to lie in the doorway while the congregation all stepped over him on the way out. As he wrote shortly afterwards, 'Not even monkeys could exhibit to the eyes of the world such shocking actions or more ridiculous behavior' (Nadler, 1999: 72). It was more than he could bear. A few days later, after finishing his autobiography, he killed himself.

Spinoza grew up in the community that experienced all this and he would have heard it all told and retold. Nevertheless he was daring enough to begin to develop notions that would have been deemed heretical. He must have begun to work on the ideas that were later published as *A Short Treatise on God, Man and His Well-Being*. In this he argued that the personal soul perishes with the body and therefore there is 'nothing to hope for or fear in terms of eternal reward or punishment' and in fact 'the notion of God acting as a free judge who dispenses reward and punishment is based on an absurd anthropomorphizing' (Nadler, 1999: 131). Although none of his writings had been published, by the time he was 23 his ideas alone seem to have brought down on his head the most extreme *cherem* that exceeds all others in its vehemence and fury (Nadler, 1999: 127):

> Cursed be he by day and cursed be he by night; cursed be he when he lies down and cursed be he when he rises up. Cursed be he when he goes out and cursed be he when he comes in ... no one shall communicate with him, either in writing, nor accord him any favor nor stay with him under the same roof nor come within four

cubits in his vicinity; nor shall he read any treatise composed or written by him ...

(Nadler, 1999: 120)

Spinoza refused to recant so was cut off for the rest of his life from his family and Jewish friends. He became a lens grinder to earn a living and wrote the *Ethics* and the *Theological-Political Treatise*, 'one of the most eloquent arguments for a secular, democratic state in the history of political thought' (285). The Synod of South Holland concluded that it was 'as vile a book as the world has ever seen' (296). Spinoza was the first philosopher to proclaim democracy as the best form of government (Israel, 2010: 94). He argued for a pantheistic outlook where God *is* the universe, a monist perspective as opposed to Descartes's dualism and arguably a materialist standpoint. His personal integrity was exemplified when the statesman Johan de Witt was accused of military incompetence after the French entered Utrecht. De Witt's brother was arrested and while the statesman was visiting him in prison a crowd broke in and dragged the two brothers off to be hanged. On the way they were beaten and killed and their bodies literally ripped apart and, allegedly, eaten by the crowd (Damasio, 2003: 21). The riot passed Spinoza's lodging and he had to be locked in by his friend and landlord to stop him going out with a placard reading '*ultimi barbarorum*' (you are the greatest barbarians). He refused generous offers of pensions from benefactors, although he finally accepted a smaller one, insisting that the original amount offered was too high. He refused the offer of the Chair of Philosophy at the University of Heidelberg because he did not want to lose study time by teaching; also he was afraid of censorship once in such a position. He died at the age of 45, probably from inhaling the dust from his lens grinding. He is understandably regarded as the philosopher's philosopher.

Rousseau is familiar to educationalists and usually derided by drama teachers who disparage Slade's drama teaching as 'Rousseauesque'. However, there is much to admire. His mother died shortly after giving birth and he was brought up by his father and an aunt. When he was ten his father fled to Switzerland to escape the law after getting into a row with a landowner, taking Rousseau's sister with him, but virtually abandoning Rousseau who made his own way in the world from then on. He was an autodidact, wandering Europe, and by the age of 30 had been 'an engraver, apprentice, domestic servant, seminarian, music teacher, interpreter for an itinerant monk, land office clerk, tutor, unsuccessful composer' and secretary to an ambassador (Damrosch, 2007: 182). His *Émile*, while surely romantic, was also a revolutionary document on child rearing. His intention was to show how a person might prepare for life without sacrificing integrity 'seeing with his own eyes, feeling with his own heart, and governed by no authority except his own reason' (Damrosch, 2007: 334). He believed in teaching by questioning and banishing fear in the pupil. Because he dared to append his own name to the book without first securing approval from the censor, the book was seized, shredded and publicly burned and a warrant issued for his arrest. Rousseau was the only writer in Europe who was systematically expelled from one country after another (418). His book *The Social Contract* inspired a generation of revolutionaries. The phrase in it 'that the people are the sovereign in every state, and ... their rights are inalienable' went almost word for word into Thomas Jefferson's 'We hold these truths to be self-evident, that all men are created equal, that they are endowed ... with certain inalienable rights' (*Declaration of Independence*). By the time of the French Revolution, Rousseau's words that we are all born equal, clearly not true, had been changed by those drawing up the constitution to 'Men are born and remain free and equal in rights. Social distinctions can be based only upon public utility.'

Voltaire, on the other hand, had a privileged upbringing and private tutors. He was a famous scholar who wrote some 15 million words. He believed in human free will and human action and saw the Christian church as a sort of 'imposture ... a con trick by which the masses were terrified into craven subjection by lies and contradictions' (Pearson, 2005: 59). He condemned the whole of French social, political, economic and intellectual life as inimical to freedom, tolerance and – interestingly – prosperity (103). Before the age of 20 he was exiled and then imprisoned in the Bastille for his satirical poems and fables. To recover some standing he changed his birth name, Arouet, to Voltaire. He spent another spell in the Bastille and spent most of his life getting ready to evade the censors or living just outside France. Much of his work was burned by the censors (there were over seventy in France) but he became very rich through colonial trade (including the slave trade), the arms trade and money lending (Pearson, 2005: 213, 229), had many servants, six horses and four carriages and believed passionately in the monarchy. His ideas were for the educated classes rather than the masses. He was not your philosopher's philosopher!

Rousseau and Voltaire could be classed as belonging to the moderate wing of the Enlightenment, d'Holbach and Diderot to the radical. Both the latter offered clear justification for mass armed resistance to tyrannical government, which view was rejected by Kant and outraged Voltaire (Israel,

2010: 86). Kant tried to bridge the two wings but finally made his peace with Frederick the Great. Kant, however, provides a clarion call for independent thinking and judgement:

> *Enlightenment is man's emergence from his self-incurred immaturity. Immaturity* is the inability to use one's own understanding without the guidance of another. This immaturity is *self-incurred* if its cause is not lack of understanding, but lack of resolution and courage to use it without the guidance of another. The motto of enlightenment is therefore: *Sapere aude!* [Dare to be wise!] Have courage to use your own understanding!
>
> (Kant, 2009: 1)

I cannot finish these tiny sketches of some of the leading figures of the Enlightenment without returning to Thomas Paine, one of the most extraordinary of these thinkers, and more of a campaigner than most. The son of a stay (corset) maker, he had no formal education. He started work at the age of 13 and became a master stay-maker but his business collapsed. Benjamin Franklin, who he met in London, wrote him a letter of recommendation and suggested he went to America. Paine did so and became a journalist. His pamphlet, *Common Sense*, urging American independence from England sold over 500,000 copies. In 1779 Congress appointed him Secretary to the Committee for Foreign Affairs but he was forced to resign after exposing embezzlement by a member of Congress. After the American Revolution Paine was left penniless as he had refused to make money from his publications. He returned to England where he was enraged at the opposition to the French Revolution and wrote the *Rights of Man*, which was highly successful and went to eight editions. It was banned, Paine was indicted for treason and an order went out for his arrest, but he had already left for France.

Paine was given honorary French citizenship and elected to the National Convention (the fiery 'parliament' of the Revolution). Paine always argued his own position and opposed the execution of the king. He fell out of favour and was arrested and sent to the guillotine. Before his arrest he had written *The Age of Reason*, an 'advocacy of deism, calling for "free rational inquiry" into all subjects, especially religion' (Marks, 2011). Those who were to be guillotined the next day had a chalk mark put on their cell doors. The door to Paine's cell had been left open to let in a little air as Paine was ill and so, as all cell doors open outwards, the mark was put on the inside of the door. During the night, other prisoners in the cell closed the door thus hiding the mark and Paine was overlooked. Eventually he was released and readmitted to the Convention after Robespierre himself was executed. At first Paine supported Napoleon but began to condemn him as the 'completest charlatan ever' (Marks, 2011). He eventually returned to America and died in poverty. He retained his principles and fought corruption to the day he died. Only six people attended his funeral.

Why are these sketches important? I want to show what we have lost in today's world. When describing the context of our work as teachers in Part One I tried to outline the present crisis in culture as the greatest problem – greater than the economic crisis, which is only a manifestation of the cultural crisis. We no longer have these thinkers dedicating every nerve to human betterment and willing to sacrifice their lives for justice. Where is our Goya? As Robert Hughes sets out in his magnificent *Goya*, 'Vietnam was tearing the country apart, and where was the art that recorded America's anguish? ... there was nothing, absolutely nothing, that came near the achievement of Goya's *Desastres de la Guerra* [Disasters of War], those heartrending prints in which the artist bore witness to the almost unspeakable facts of death in the Spanish rising against Napoleon' (Hughes, 2003: 7). The same question could be asked about the horrors of the Iraq War and other wars and atrocities with which our epoch is littered. Instead of Goya we have Tracey Emin's *My Bed* or Damien Hirst's diamond skull.

The Enlightenment received its death sentence with the Congress of Vienna in 1814 where the ambassadors of Europe came together after the defeat of Napoleon to forge an alliance of constitutional monarchies and existing monarchs to make sure there were no more people's revolutions. Beethoven's Ninth Symphony can be seen as a last cry for the Enlightenment and universal brotherhood and sisterhood. As Barenboim says of Beethoven, '[He] must have been an extraordinarily interesting human being. He understood independence of thought was the greatest gift one could have on earth – more than fame, material gain – the ability to really think this is right and this is wrong and this is the way I want to live' (Barenboim, 2012). We could equally ask – Where are our Beethovens now?

However, reason devoid of human values can be a dangerous thing, a fact that was already acknowledged in the Age of Reason when Rousseau warned against 'pure' reason: 'Rousseau, it is true, complicated matters by questioning the superiority of reason over feeling ... reason is not necessarily to be trusted: it can be the source of duplicity and vanity, of political repression and a singular lack of fraternity' (Pearson, 2005: 70). And Goya's etching *The Sleep of Reason* shows a figure (perhaps Goya himself?) slumped asleep on his table with owls and bats flying above him. In Spain at that time owls and bats were symbols of unreason, of ignorance and mindless stupidity. His full title for the etching is 'Imagination abandoned by reason produces impossible monsters: united with her, she is the mother of the arts and the source of her wonders'. The title in Spanish is *El sueño de la razón*. This is interesting, as the Spanish *sueño* means sleep but also dream. This has led to speculation that Goya was saying that reason can dream up ignorance and stupidities if separated from imagination and likewise for imagination if it is separated from reason. I like to think this is what Goya intended. It is certainly Bond's pursuit in his drama, on which more below.

What marked out the reasoning of the Enlightenment was the value system at its core. It was all focused on seeking a better, more humane, more just way of sharing the planet together. As Saul (1993) points out in his aptly named *Voltaire's Bastards*, 'Were Voltaire to reappear today, he would be outraged by the new structures, which somehow deformed the changes for which he had struggled' (Saul, 1993: 5). Reason has now become functional administration and the administration is one of neo-liberal values or worse. We are witnessing the 'conversion of Western civilization to a methodology devoid of values' (18).

Bond, Brecht and Bolton

> I think I grew up to be a writer because I had the ability to be completely involved in my experience but at the same time to be an observer of it (which is what accident time is).
>
> (Bond, 2013b)

It would be false to think that Bond is not pursuing reason. Bond and Brecht have the same goals: the development of a form of drama/theatre that will open people's eyes to the 'reality' in which they are immersed. They both want to put human value back into reason. They are both taking a stand against 'authority', if by authority is meant the ideas of a culture that dominate and take over people's thinking: the dominant ideology or ideologies of a culture. However the routes they have chosen to achieve this are diametrically opposed in important ways. Brecht sought to depersonalize the relationship between the audience and the play. He developed a form of theatre that aimed to stop the audience becoming engaged in the story that enmeshed the characters in the drama; to stop them empathizing with the characters' dilemmas and struggles; to force the audience to sit back and take a long, hard rational look at what was taking place. To do this he developed devices such as montage, *gestus*, the not-but, an episodic form to break up the story and a demonstrating style of acting. Bond, on the other hand, as the quotation heading this section describes, is concerned to involve the audience in the story, engage them in a feeling way with the problems the characters face, but also enable the audience to observe what is happening at the same time: being in the stream with them, not outside looking on. This is the link between Bond and Bolton. It is the *immediacy* of the relationship with the event that is key. For Bolton it is a *metaxis* form of involvement in the drama event taken to its extreme and for Bond it is the audience using its imagination *and* reason in *accident time*. (Bond's terms are set out with explanations below.) For both Bolton and Bond, it involves a visceral, affective immersion in the event leading to imaginative/reasoned reflection. This is sufficient for Bolton but not for Bond; here they separate and new elements come in.[1] Bolton is content for the present ideological understanding of the participants to be enough for them to reflect on the events and their involvement in them. And Brecht believed his drama devices did enough to enable the audience to see clearly the real forces at work in society. Bond does not accept that this is what happens. He argues that in Brecht's theatre the audience is left blindfolded. For Bond the challenge is how the engagement of the audience with the drama event can enable them to see what is really happening, to think with the eyes, as he says somewhere, without the event being cloaked in the immediate understanding of ideology. With regard to Bolton, my proposal is that although his drama form stays with the importance of story, does not pursue distancing devices and works for *metaxis*, yet the participants' *being* is still enmeshed in their dominant ideology, whatever that is.

Bond is quite specific about his differences with Brecht and much of his theoretical writing is devoted to attempting to clarify how his drama works and how it is different to Brecht's.

> It is necessary for me to elucidate why I am not a Brechtian – and cannot be if I am to write of my times. And so I have to make clear why I cannot be: and that means not dismissing Brecht but arguing that he belongs to a now redundant paradigm of knowledge. I take alienation from within the act – I do not apply it. I do not have to alienate *Coffee* – from within the centre of the drama the alienated may be made to reveal itself as fact – the coffee cup (and so I have had to create the TE [Theatre Event]). I achieve 'specification' – I specify what is happening – so that it cannot be ideologically cloaked (without a deliberate effort of denial by the audience).
>
> (Bond, 2000: 173)

The reference to the cup is from his play *Coffee* (Bond, 1995a). In part of that play soldiers have been 'working' hard all day, machine-gunning civilian prisoners who have to be 'disposed' of. (It is taken from a real incident at Babi Yar, a ravine in the Ukraine where 33,771 Jews from the city of Kiev were killed by the Nazis in a single operation. Other victims massacred at the site included thousands of Soviet prisoners of war, communists, Romani gypsies, Ukrainian nationalists and civilian hostages. It is estimated that between 100,000 and 150,000 lives were taken at Babi Yar.)

In the play the soldiers speak demotic English but their nationality is not specified. They drink coffee, not tea, and schnapps. The prisoners have to walk along a narrow path in the side of a ravine. When they are shot the bodies fall into a ready prepared grave – the ravine. The soldiers/workers think they have come to the end of their shift when the order comes that some more prisoners have been found in the back of a lorry. They are just about to have a coffee break, which they feel they have worked hard for and deserve, and the coffee has been brewing in the background. It is a bit like having a picnic out in the country while also 'working' at killing people. One of the soldiers throws the coffee out of the jug.

Why? The act of throwing out the coffee does not need 'alienating'. The action of flinging the coffee across the ground (in fact across the stage with a 'whoosh' according to the stage directions) itself has the potential to disturb the audience into a new way of 'seeing' what is happening, of disturbing their ideological perspective whatever that might be and reaching out to their human 'being'. The reference to TE (Theatre Event) is Bond's term for creating that drama moment. He now calls it a Drama Event (DE) as he has sought to distance his form of drama from conventional theatre with its showy effects as described in the early part of this book. I think he uses the term 'alienation' (in the quotation above) to connect with his critique of Brecht but would now disavow the use of the term and perhaps speak of evoking imagination/reason in one moment of accident time, where apperception is heightened through the extreme moment. As happens in an accident, the mind works so fast that things seem to happen slowly so that all the details can be apprehended. There is no intention to produce a common reaction. Rather he intends to create the possibility to think with the eyes. One member of the audience might be disturbed by the splashing of dark liquid across the stage and viscerally connect it with blood being spilled. Another might feel in this action an act of autonomy, of self-assertion. It might lead her to wonder how the soldiers have been corrupted, how their humanity has been crushed by obedience, turning them into slaves who think they still have autonomy as they argue with the Sergeant about not going back to work. This might lead her to reflect on how she has succumbed to blind obedience in her own work. Another audience member might be reminded of how he hated the NCOs and the officers when in the forces. Another might empathize with the soldiers. As Bond describes it:

> Theatre dramatizes imagination in small, seemingly insignificant incidents, and in incidents of obvious significance. Drama cannot instruct, it confronts, perplexes and intrigues imagination into recreating reality. ... Its confrontations force some people deeper into reaction, but then they must take responsibility for it and cannot leave it to authority.
>
> (Bond, 1995a: xxxiv)

Drama offers a means to pierce the mantle of ideology that cloaks us all.

Ideology

What does Bond mean by ideology? In trying to paraphrase Bond's many detailed writings in this area, I risk over-simplification and misrepresentation. However, I must try.

Initially, I intended to survey major interpretations of the meaning of ideology in order to contextualize Bond's approach. Having got as far as Žižek (2008) and Hawkes (2003) only to find that Eagleton (2007) alone puts forward 16 meanings of the term, I gave up. There is neither the space nor is it strictly necessary to define the term here, even if I could. I am afraid Alan Greenspan will have to do to introduce the concept.

Greenspan was Chairman of the Federal Reserve in the United States from 1987 to 2006. He had the stewardship of the US economy for 19 years. When the economy crashed he was called before a Congressional Committee hearing in 2008 to be questioned about what had gone wrong. As part of his testimony he said:

> Remember what an ideology is. It's a conceptual framework of the way people deal with reality. Everyone has one. You have to – to exist you need an ideology. The question is whether it is accurate or not. And what I am saying to you is yes, I have found a flaw – I don't know how significant or permanent it is but I've been very distressed by that flaw ... a flaw in the model that I perceived is the critical functioning structure that defines how the world works, so to speak.
>
> (www.pbs.org/newshour/bb/business/july-dec08/
> crisishearing_10-23.html)

One is almost tempted to feel sorry for him. The financial world would not behave as he thought it should, as his ideology told him it would.

The part of his explanation that seems to fit is the all-pervasive nature of ideology. Humans are self-conscious and need to make meanings: to understand themselves in relation to the material world and to other people. All social groups throughout human history and prehistory have found ways to explain themselves to themselves, sometimes through myth and legend, and sometimes through science, as Stephen Hawking does in the quotation which opens Part Three. The part of Greenspan's explanation that does not seem accurate is his sense of it being a personal question, as though we make up our own ideology as an individual intellectual act. For Bond, 'Ideology is the meaning society gives to itself, reality and so to "being"' (Bond, 2000: 175). There are three important components here. There is social reality, physical reality and human 'being', which is 'on the border between ideology and practical knowledge of reality' (175).

Bond is a materialist so he sees everything in the universe as made up of matter – from people to the bullets and guns that kill them. However, there is also imagination that resides in our 'being' and is not bound to matter but able to explore the meaning of the natural and the social and bring value to reasoning. It is through imagination interconnected with reason that we explain ourselves to ourselves. Once human society divided into classes, society became unjust. The explanations then came from the voices of authority or their servants and these invented reasons explained and justified authority's domination. These voices of authority become ideology in its various protean forms and guises. However, our human 'being' is also the source of a creative opposition to authority. The artist and the philosopher can imagine another way of understanding ourselves that can open a path to a more human future. Picasso can paint *Guernica*, Shakespeare can write *King Lear,* and a child can watch people out of a window and wonder.

Bond sees our 'being' as living in the gap or space between practical, physical reality (water boils at a certain temperature, wood burns) and imagined social reality (making tea or coffee is a good way of welcoming people, we are all equal before the law). The practical reality is finally consistent and subject to laws that can be uncovered, but the social is imagined through the lens of ideology. We are not prisoners of ideology unless we desire to be or are not conscious of our imprisonment. However, our bodies are on both sides of the boundary: a social being that might believe in fairies could also have cancer. Practical reality can also be endowed with ideology – the notion that the earth was formed in six days. But this form of ideology is undermined by science over time.

The nature of our 'being' is central to Bond's drama form. He brings an original perspective to what is essential, of the essence, in human 'being'. He proposes that the newborn child strives to be at home in the world. This is its right and every human strives to achieve it. He says: 'Nothing else has the dignity of a crying child' (Bond, 1995b: xxxiv). Damasio (2003) claims that 'Feelings of pain or pleasure ... are the bedrock of our minds' (3), but Bond would argue that this is too crude. There is from the beginning an intellection, an embryonic thought process. The newborn child strives for comfort, warmth and food and struggles against cold, hunger and discomfort. Bond argues that this early striving forms a foundation for justice, for what is positive in human being, and that this remains under all the later layers of self that develop, including the layers of corruption that may be built up by later enculturation. He calls this state Radical Innocence and bases his drama on finding a way to connect with that basic striving for justice laid down in all of us so early in life. That striving for justice lays the basis for the self to be self-created rather than just socially formed. It is created in the conflict against the corruption of an ideologized society. The child has to fight against injustice to create a human self. Or as Bond himself would describe it:

> The dramatist must introspect his characters' minds. He must see them from within. This can be done even with the new born baby – the neonate. The neonate does not yet have the character of a self-identity but it cannot be reduced to its bare genetics. It is already a matter of experience. The neonate's mind is laying the foundations on which later it will build everything else. It has no concept of internal and external, of subjective and objective. Instead it takes itself to be the total of reality. The external is simply an inward-extension of itself. (In part this resembles Leibnitz's concept of the 'monad'.) We must make the imaginative leap to understand the neonate's understanding of reality because it is the opposite of our adult understanding of it. It is essential to see it from the neonate's point of view because that is how the neonate creates the foundations of our humanness. The neonate not only feels pleasure and pain, it discerns a pattern between them and this early 'act of intellect' gives reality a structure and a meaning. This is the threefold structure of the self that makes us human because it makes us *responsible* for reality, for the world. As the neonate thinks it *is* the world, then it is responsible for the

world's pleasures and pains and the meaning of reality. This is the origin of our moral sense. It is a state of radical innocence. The neonate seeks to be at home in itself, in itself-as-world. Later this becomes the imperative to justice. Already at our birth we are at the beginnings of the huge cultural structures of the Tragic and the Comic and the meaning of humanness. At first this responsibility is only for the self because the self is the entirety of all things. But then the infant learns that it shares the world with others and so its moral responsibility *must* be extended to them. *Must* – because the self is indivisibly raised on its first foundations and so morality is indivisible. But the infant will also learn that reality is mortal and we are condemned to die because we have been born. And it will soon learn that society is unjust. Mortality and injustice are the stronghold of Ideology. Ideology's explanation of reality justifies injustice and the power of life and death. This conflicts with our indivisible imperative to be human. And so society entangles and embroils morality in immorality and confounds the human imperative with the obligation to obey. It turns justice into revenge. This is the conflict at the core of drama. Drama is not a 'cultural refinement' but the core of our humanness. Unjust society's appeals to our goodwill are at best useless and at worst manipulative and inhuman. Civil war is rare, but social war is permanent. To survive as humans we must dramatise the paradox of humanness. In drama, radical innocence returns to confront its own corruption. It enters the maze of ideology and self-repression to create the logic of humanness. We are the dramatic species. This is as true of the schoolroom as it was of the Theatre of Dionysus in Athens.

(Bond, 2013e)

A way forward for all of us to be human is to work towards a state where we are all at home in the world.

To contribute to this process Bond's drama form strives to connect with this basic striving for justice we have all created in ourselves so early in life. He does this by finding ways to open a door on what we are doing to each other or rather, how society's forces, its ideologies, influence and take over our understanding of our personal and social relations. The drama needs to be so structured that it asks of the audience 'Who are we?' and to do this needs to make a primary connection with the audience's imagination rather than a primary connection with reason. He argues that 'Reason alone cannot help us to understand our situation humanly, or even use ideology against ideology' (Bond, 2000: 179). This is because reason may already be corrupted by ideology but 'imagination cannot be corrupted because it has no ideas' (181). I think he means by this, that although imagination and reason are intertwined, imagination has no ideas intrinsic to it as a faculty. The ideas are in reason and memory, which are in dialectical unity with imagination. By primarily evoking imagination, his drama seeks to make the audience subjects, rather than objects, so they are 'creators of meanings' (Bond, 2000: 18).

The next section outlines the basics of the drama theory structured into Bond's plays: theory that sets out to achieve the connections described.

Notes
[1] Here I should also align my own approach with Bolton's as I closely follow key dimensions of Bolton's work as demonstrated in my process drama above. My approach is up for review, however, later in this section.

Chapter 7

Bondian drama

(with Chris Cooper)

The rest of this book is written in close collaboration with Chris Cooper, Artistic Director of Big Brum Theatre in Education Company. Chris Cooper has had a close collaboration with Edward Bond over some 18 years. Big Brum has commissioned ten plays from Edward Bond during this time and the author has attended at least some of the rehearsals of each play and helped shape the direction of them.[1] He has also seen all the plays in performance, some of them several times, in both the UK and abroad. This makes it a unique collaboration, the only one of its kind that Bond has in the UK, where he works with a professional company from commission, through rehearsals, to performance. It means that the world premiere of a new Bond play often takes place in a primary or secondary school in Birmingham with a single class of children. The result is that Cooper is uniquely placed as a collaborator for this section. There is no one in the UK who knows more about how Bond's plays work in practice and theory. I have followed his notes closely but have not referenced each of them as this would negate the idea of our collaboration in the writing.

Components of Bondian drama
In Kostas Amoiropoulos's extremely interesting PhD (2013), he presents a perceptive study of Bond's theory and a detailed examination of the rehearsal process of one of Bond's plays for Big Brum, *A Window*. Amoiropoulos isolates nine key components of Bond's theatre form, of his theatre aesthetic. Cooper and I have agreed that these would make a useful starting point to assemble an alternative list of components to those I propose for process drama in Part Two. They are, in no particular order: **story, site, centre, enactment, cathexis, extreme, accident time, drama event** and the **invisible object**. I venture to add the **gap** to this list. Each of these is set out below with explanations and each is exemplified in moments from one of Bond's plays, *The Broken Bowl*. This play was premiered by Big Brum and directed by Chris Cooper. An outline of the play is given first and then each of the components is described in relation to the play.

The Broken Bowl

This is a play for 9–12 year olds and is set in a room, in a city where the family lives. It is set 'Towards the year 2077', with society crumbling outside the door. Inside, a family gathers to eat the only food available, dry muesli. The family consists of a mother, a father and their daughter who is about the same age as the audience. The play takes place over three mealtimes.

One

The set is simple. 'At the back a plain wall. In the middle of it a door that leads to the street. A window to the left of the door. [Stage right.] The kitchen is off to the right. [Stage left.] A wooden table and four wooden chairs. Three chairs are set at the table. The fourth chair stands against the wall. On the table three low-sided pink bowls and three plastic spoons' (Unpublished script).

Mother calls the family to the table. Father appears and sits. The daughter is late. She excuses herself as she brings the fourth chair to the table. Father objects, mother attempts to mollify him. Daughter brings in an extra bowl, mauve, and pours muesli into it. She has an imaginary friend. She puts a cushion on his chair to make him more comfortable. Her father throws it to the floor, making her cry. Mother tries to defend her again. The row increases. The father goes to take the bowl but the mother stops him. A blast of wind rattles the windows. The father looks out but can see nothing. The bowls are cleared away. The father takes a step towards the fourth chair but turns away.

Two

Mother sets the table with bowls and the carton of muesli. Father comes in with hammer, a board and nails to board over the window to keep the wind out. He starts hammering. The mother questions it and he tells her the whole street is doing it. The daughter comes in with the extra bowl. Father complains again and mother defends her. The daughter offers to hold the nails. Father holds his hammer up for silence. He thinks he has heard something. It is nothing but he tells them how he thought he heard wolves howling in the street the previous night – but it was only some drunk young lads. He hits his thumb with the hammer and blames the girl and her 'zombie' imaginary friend. She offers to get some antiseptic lotion. He complains again about the bowl. The girl will not take it away. The father goes to the table and smashes it with his hammer, scattering the bowl and muesli on the table and the floor. The father makes the girl clear it up. He goes to pour some more food for himself but his wife stops him. There is not enough food to go round. He goes outside. He may have heard something. The girl comes in from the kitchen with a tin bowl this time. She cannot find her imaginary friend. She pleads for him to come back if he can hear her. Father comes back in to tell them they have to chop up the furniture for fuel before thieves break in and steal it – all the street is doing so. Mother protests but is gradually persuaded. They go into the kitchen with a chair each. The girl sits on the fourth chair to protect it for her friend. Father takes out the third chair and tells her he will chop the fourth chair from under her if she does not move. A blast of wind blows open the door and she goes out to look for her friend. Father comes back in, sees she has gone and eats the food she has put in the tin bowl. Father goes out to look for her. Her imaginary friend, No One, comes in. He sits on the fourth chair. The father comes back in but cannot see No One. The girl tells her father she is delighted to see her friend back and points to the empty bowl as proof of his existence. The father does not respond. She takes out his tin bowl. The father goes towards the chair to take it but does not and follows the girl into the kitchen. No One looks out of the door but goes out through the wall, the way he came in.

Three

It is cold, and a blanketed mother sets out the bowls and spoons for a muesli meal on the floor. The girl comes in also wrapped in a blanket and carrying the tin bowl. Father is still out and mother is worried. The girl goes to fill the tin bowl and for the first time her mother stops her. Her mother is now siding with the father. The father comes back in from the street. He is shaken. The street is empty. Everyone has left. He turns on the child, verbally blaming her for what has happened. It must have been her, running down the street knocking on all the doors asking for her friend. He makes her go to the door and open it. She opens it inch by inch. The door swings open and there is a 'huge, ugly dripping red X' marked on it. They sit to eat to try to conjure up normality. She is not allowed to put out food for No One, who enters, haggard, clothes torn, starving and barefoot. He accuses the girl of betraying him. The father sees him but refuses him food. The girl knocks out of her father's hand the spoon he is waving as a weapon and tramples the food into the floor saying 'if he can't eat no one can'. The father goes out into the street. Mother follows him. The girl scoops up food and tries to feed No One. The food from the floor is mixed with dirt. No One leaves. The mother returns without father who is running in the streets. She says she must go to him. The girl wraps a blanket around her mother's shoulders. The mother leaves. Another teenager enters the room through the open door. He looks like her imaginary friend but is real. The play ends with them going out together:

Girl (*touching his arm. Silence*)	We have to feed the hungry don't we.
Someone	Yes.
Girl	And feed the poor.
Someone	Yes. Something's happened in the streets. They're empty. Shall we go to see?
Girl	Yes.

(*Someone and Girl go out through the door. The room is empty. The tin bowl is on the chair.*)

Story

Story is fundamental to human self-consciousness. In daily life we hear stories everywhere: on the bus, at work, in the pub, in the gym. Wherever we meet other people we share small stories of our daily lives. These can be woven into larger cultural stories to explain ourselves to ourselves. As Bruner puts it, when teasing out the different use of imagination in rational, logical, scientific discourse and its use in story:

> The imaginative application of the narrative mode leads instead to good stories, gripping drama, believable (though not necessarily 'true') historical accounts. It deals in human or human-like intention and action and the vicissitudes and consequences that mark their course [and] it must construct two landscapes simultaneously. One is the landscape of action ... The other is the landscape of consciousness.
>
> (Bruner, 1986: 11–12)

The importance of story is central to Bond's plays. Unlike postmodern/ poststructuralist approaches to story, Bond does not break up the narrative. The strong storyline is important. It is the first way of engaging the audience with the world of the play or, rather, bringing them into the play. It is the most basic way we have of reflecting ourselves to ourselves.

In *The Broken Bowl* a father, acting from fear of what he imagines is happening outside the front door, is self-destructing and intent on taking his family with him: entombing them, chopping up the furniture. His young daughter intuitively knows they need to be reaching out to others: to find solutions to the problem together. The father is driven by corrupted imagination so he becomes irrational whereas the daughter is driven by imagination that, to start with, has not yet found the rational, even though it has found a level of reasoning. Eventually she can imagine the real. 'When imagination penetrates reality the imagined is real' (Bond, 2000: 49). The mother starts by mediating between the two and then succumbs to her husband's pressure. The girl finally reaches a stage where she is able to break free from the prison her father is trying to lock her in, and find an actual friend. She takes charge of the situation, puts a blanket around her mother's shoulders as though her mother were the child, and the girl and Someone (the new person she meets) go out to seek others, to try to find solutions together. Told like this it remains a moral tale; a tale told in ideology.

It is the drama devices that Bond employs that deconstruct the story and make it possible to reach round behind the ideology. The story itself is never broken but is structured in such a way that there are opportunities to open the story to analysis without it losing its grip. An imaginary friend, at first only in the girl's imagination, begins to become alive for the rest of us. The more the personal, irrational actions of the father dominate, the more we come to see just how drastic a state the imaginary friend is in: 'haggard, dirty, starving, in rags and barefoot'. Having reduced himself to his most desperate state of 'madness', the father also sees No One. A subconscious part of him knows his daughter is right. He glimpses his own humanness and it terrifies him. As with many of Bond's plays the storyline in the play seems straightforward but then situations arise when the story is taken in seemingly different directions. We can understand the child having an imaginary friend, and even accept that we can see what the girl sees, but what is happening when the father also sees No One? That is perplexing – and without breaking the story our imaginations are forced into overdrive. The play and its performance need to be structured in such a way that the story is opened for analysis without breaking the narrative drive. How this is done will be the subject of the rest of this section.

There is a danger in isolating the drama components. It can make it seem as though they are ingredients and all that is needed is to add each one and you have a Bond play in performance. It is necessary to isolate them as part of the analysis but they combine and interact just as Brecht's, Bolton's and Heathcote's do in their own ways, and doing that combining is a creative, artistic process. As with any creative artist, I suspect playwrights do not start writing plays fully understanding their craft, but as they write, the plays teach them what they are doing. The understanding and the creating are intertwined, with the creating leading the process not vice versa. This is surely true of Bond. I have seen him watching a rehearsal of one of his plays, scrutinizing the script as though it were written by someone else, and speculating afresh on why the characters are doing what they are, and how they might do it.

Site

Of key importance in the list of drama components is Bond's understanding of the site of the drama. 'The site is the self in its total situation. Self and society, psychology and politics, belong to the site' (Bond, 2000: 48). He identifies four interacting sites in drama:

A. It conforms to the social sites (city, era, culture etc.), which are self-evident to the audience.
B. It conveys to the audience the play's specific sites. These are equivalent to A but may of course be different.
C. It conveys the play to the audience – the audience *as* site. The audience is social, able to receive only in certain (if sometimes innovative) ways. C must convey A and B to the audience.
D. The audience as site of imagination. A, B and C must be conveyed to this site. D is drama's *specific* site because – through the play – it contains all the other sites and their interrelations. What is D? What is the need for drama? Drama's identity comes from meeting the needs of D.

(Bond, 2000: 10)[2]

How do these work out in *The Broken Bowl?*

Site A, the social site, is apparent in the panic outside in the streets, the fear, the wind (an ecological or nuclear disaster maybe), the food shortage and the famine figure who appears at the end of the play, No One. He is the first glimpse we get of the 'actual' social world in which the room sits. Site A has become the site of disaster.

Site B, the specific site of the play, has two dimensions to it: the story, what happens in that social context, and its location, a room in a house. The story shows us what happens in the play but does not explain it. The play is written to provide key moments when a gap can be made for meaning making. Its location, a sparsely furnished living/dining area, demonstrates the functionality of the few things in it. The simplicity of the room underlines the key importance of design for Bond. 'Design is at the centre of my plays and if the design isn't right the play can't work – that is why some productions by schools with no money for design work better than expensive productions in large theatres' (Bond, 2000: 51). Site A invades Site B. It swings into the room as the cross on the door. It rattles the window panes. It leads to the destruction of the furniture and the father to smash the bowl as Site A invades his mind. The social context is exemplified in the plain muesli carton, the bareness of the room – not a glimpse of holiday mementos or souvenirs. For the young people the point is being made that you can only change your situation meaningfully when you can change Site A.

Site C, how the play is conveyed to the audience, is central to the whole process. The actors and directors, as creative artists, play a key role in the performance of Bond's plays. Directors, actors and their teachers at drama schools and universities have neither taken the trouble to understand the theory behind Bond's plays nor how to carry it out in practice. They are still immersed in Stanislavski, Brecht or other Performance Theatre modes and do not realize that a Bond play will not respond to these approaches and their methods. It is one of the reasons why he has become disillusioned with British theatre.[3] In Site C you have the special attention given to *objects* and how they are *cathected* and *de-cathected* in a Bond play, along with the means to open out the *centre* of the play to reveal the *invisible object*. The centre is made available through doors opened by *drama events* that contain the *extreme* moments in the story, which are played out in *accident time*. All these depend on how the play is *enacted*. Each of these components is opened out below in relation to the play. In other words, Site C is *how* the story of the play is turned into something that can engage with and energize the creative imagination of the audience.

Site D is the audience as the site of imagination. It is the site of the existential and the social self, made available for re-evaluation through opening out the interaction of the existential self with the social self, embodied in the play and its performance. This seems complicated but if there were not an existential self, continually able to recreate itself, then we would be social zombies, owned by authority. It is where we, the audience, become part of the play and have the chance to meet ourselves as ourselves. We may not recognize each other, of course, and that is the option that Bond always invites. As Bond puts it:

> I've said that the play takes place in the actor's mind but also
> in the audience's mind – they become one: the audience *are* the
> stage. And so they recognise themselves, or their knowledge and
> experience, in the actors in the situation – they don't become the
> actors but recognise themselves in them and also, because the stage
> is a forensic reality, they are confirmed in their own need to know,
> they enjoy the 'conventionality' of the cultural method because it

can also show them the reality of their own experience – they enjoy the creative skills in the stage work of art – so they 'enjoy' both the *purpose* of drama and what it creates. And this confirms for them, instantiates it, that they are creators of their own experience, and ultimately this enables the victim to become the agent of power and change. If the actors can understand the situation and enter it completely then – when they reach the drama's centre – they will find the audience waiting for them (and the audience will find the actor–characters).

(Bond, 2013d)

Centre

Bond argues that every worthwhile play has a centre and there will indeed be a central line. This centre would need to permeate every scene, every action of the play in performance. Any production team would have to find a centre that is relevant to their time, audience, culture, location and so on. It is not given by the author of a play. If we take Shakespeare's *The Merchant of Venice*, for example, it could be legitimate to take as the centre the importance of the bond in Venetian society, and in any commercial society. The play echoes with bonds: given to Shylock, given between lovers, given by daughters to fathers. The central speech that might be chosen is that spoken by Antonio after trying to speak to Shylock about the bond (taking a pound of flesh as payment for the debt). Antonio is already in prison and has bribed the gaoler to let him out to speak to Shylock but Shylock will have none of it. Salarino, Antonio's friend, tries to reassure Antonio that the Duke will side with him and not Shylock. Antonio answers:

> The duke cannot deny the course of law:
> For the commodity that strangers have
> With us in Venice, if it be denied,
> Will much impeach the justice of his state;
> Since that the trade and profit of the city
> Consisteth of all nations.

(*The Merchant of Venice*, IV, iii)

A human solution in the form of mercy has no place in commerce; 'the trade and profit of the city' are the overriding concerns. Law, justice and mercy do not mix: gold is all. And even more so for the merchants and rulers of the city state than for the Jew who is only their servant money-lender and follows the code set up by his masters. This might legitimately be the centre of the play for a production team and the above speech the central speech with a possible central line.

In *The Broken Bowl* the company (Big Brum TiE):

> defined the centre ... as an exploration of how fear and isolation impact on our perception of the real and the imagined. This became the centre of 'our play' and the starting point from which to build a programme to which the children could bring their own life and meanings. The TIE programme was then structured accordingly.
>
> (Cooper, 2013: 135)

The central line chosen was one of the girl's lines spoken to her imaginary friend, 'My dad's afraid of you'. The imaginary friend stands in the father's eye for all that is collapsing outside the front door, all that terrifies him. We never find out what has really happened 'outside' and we do not need to. Society has long since collapsed. People try to survive in isolated families. The sense of powerlessness and isolation is brought in from outside. We hear of the long queues even for muesli. The father's reports that other people are boarding up their windows (building their own coffins) and chopping up and burning their furniture (destroying the last remnants of the rain forests) lead him desperately to follow suit. Young people are drinking themselves silly as the *Titanic* sinks – that is social madness. These are all images that resonate with how we are living now, with our insane rush to the cliff edge.

This centre pervades every moment of the play and informs how it needs to be not acted but rather, as Bond would say, enacted.

Enactment

Enactment needs to resonate the chosen central concerns of the play, not the individual actor's skill at character acting. For example, the way in which the girl first brings in the mauve bowl for her imaginary friend can be done in a whole range of ways. If she were to *act* it in a Stanislavskian way the actor might be trying to find the part of her character that is independent, strong, resilient and so on. But to *enact* it might involve the carrying having some sense of the desperate plight of those who have no food at all, but done without any show of sentimentality. It is just a young girl who senses there are others to feed and cannot verbalize it but projects it into her 'play'. As with the way the father bangs in the nails to board up the windows, this could be done stemming just from an 'interpretation' of the father as a stereotypical dominant male. Alternatively the violent hammering by the father as he entombs his family, impelled by his imagined fear of the wind but really of the people outside (including their neighbours), could have the sense of a 'good' man attempting to protect his family but driven to panicky insane acts by his corrupted imagination/reasoning. In this enactment the psychological is not banished but is coherent with the centre and expands it and draws the audience of young people into the family's predicament. Many of the young children will have experienced a dominant father figure acting in ways he sees as best for the family or the child in question, but really acting illogically. 'If you don't keep your room tidy, your mum and I are going to leave the kitchen in a complete mess to show you what it is like to live in a pigsty.' And in the play, the smashing of the bowl with food in it, when they are down to their last few possessions, becomes madness in the name of reason.

Cathexis (mainly of objects)

The way Bond uses objects is key to his drama form. He does not use them as symbols – quite the opposite. He chooses everyday objects that do not hold a symbolic significance in the culture. In *The Broken Bowl* he chooses bowls, a hammer, a hatchet, a chair and so on. Because they do not have significance attached to them as they would if they were symbols, they can be invested with significance, cathected, to borrow a term from Freud. However, Bond does not focus its usage, as Freud does on the projection of libidinal energy into an object, but uses it in a wider way to describe the individual feelings and values embedded in an object, usually by one of the characters in the play. When the girl brings in her mauve bowl for her imaginary friend she has endowed it with special significance for herself. It is a warm spot in an icy world. She has cathected it. When the father smashes the bowl it is de-cathected and the pieces scattered. Objectively, he is attempting to destroy her imagination, her humanness; subjectively, he sees himself saving the family from madness. The bowl reappears, this time as a tin bowl, and is re-cathected with even more determination and affect. I think the tin bowl would need to be carefully chosen. The wrong sort of bowl, say a certain sort of battered tin bowl, might conjure up prisoners or prisoners of war. Then it would become a symbol and would take over the audience's imagination so it would need to be an ordinary kitchen utensil, recognizable as such. The bowl is de-cathected again when the father eats out of it. He sees zombies, and the girl sees the future of humanity. The bowl journeys through the play. At one stage the girl is forbidden to put muesli from the packet into the bowl, so she pours into it half of her own, re-cathecting it. The father empties it out, de-cathecting it again. Fundamentally different values and attitudes towards the future of humanity are being played out. The same analysis could be made of all the different objects used in the play.

Extreme

Bond pushes moments in the drama to extremes. In real life we enter extreme moments when we have to find out who we are. It provides an opportunity to separate the real from under an ideological cloud. Malala Yousafzai, shot by the Taliban for speaking out about girls' right to education, was shot by a young man. The teenager's profound comment about the young man who shot her afterward was 'It's hard to have a gun and kill people. Maybe that's why his hand was shaking' (*Guardian* headline, 8 October 2013). Here we see imagination filled with human values leading reason: imagining the real. Or let us say, a hit and run driver mows down a child. It is an extreme moment in the parents' lives. They can be driven to revenge and hatred, destroying humanness, or they can cling on to humanness however difficult this is to do, and realize that to destroy another human being will not bring back a loved one but only in the end be self-destructive. In every Bond play there are moments taken to extremes. Two of the most obvious in *The Broken Bowl* are the smashing of the bowl and the very slow opening of the door to reveal the cross. The enactment of such moments creates a drama event.

Drama event

Several of Bond's drama components come together in a drama event. It aims to create *accident time* and a *gap* to reveal *the invisible object*. These are really inseparable so will be explored together. A drama event deconstructs the story and prevents it from being told in ideology. It takes key moments in the play, usually extreme moments, and the way they are enacted opens up that situation for the audience to enter and face the reality of the situation. They cannot just sit back and follow the story any more. The revealing of the cross on the door is such a moment.

The tension of forcing the girl to open the door is built inexorably and painfully:

Father	Open the door.
Girl	No. – Mum he's going to send me away – ! [A truly terrifying prospect and a child's deepest fear – of abandonment.]
Father	Open the door.
Mother	I can't help you anymore. [Her mother has abandoned her.]

Father	(To Mother) I didn't want you to see this. [Father protecting the mother and terrifying the daughter.] (To Girl) Open it.
	(Girl goes to the door. She opens it a fraction. Stands there) [We cannot see what is outside and nor can she.]
Father	Open it. (She opens it further) Wider. (She opens it further. Peers through the crack) Wider.
	(The girl goes limp – the door falls open. The outside of the door is painted with a huge ugly dripping red X. Girl steps back into the room. Mother stares in shock.)

The father, even after this, turns the screw another turn:

Father	They've marked our house. We're lepers. The cold. The broken windows. Doors blown in. Roofs collapsing. Furniture burnt. Starvation. Looters and wreckers. A ghost town! They have to blame someone so they're blaming us! (Eats. To Mother) Shut it. She's seen it.
Mother	(Shuts the door) You've dragged us down to this. . . What can we do?

It is as extreme a moment as could be made with 9–12 year olds. When I saw the performance there was a palpable gasp from the children. Such a moment Bond would refer to as potentially creating *accident time*. As in an accident, to protect the body the brain moves so fast that things seem to slow down.

Accident time

Accident time is another important component of Bond's drama theory. It can be misleading to think of accident time as purely a biological phenomenon. For Bond it is a way of describing what happens in a drama event. All the dimensions of the *centre* come together in an extreme moment or situation. It is in extreme events that we tend to find ideology at its strongest and clearest and therefore it is a useful place to confront it. The slow opening of the door to reveal the cross brings the madness of the social world (already invading the father) into the room. If the actors have enacted the situation, that is, brought the centre of the play strongly into focus, then the power of drama is brought into action. The audience, young people in this case, can *see* what is happening. They are not being told it. They can judge for themselves what is happening. Thus the key dimensions of Bond's drama form described earlier come into play. The drama seeks to connect with the audience's Radical Innocence, that basic striving for justice laid down in all of us early in life. This evokes the audience's imagination to work out what is actually going on, the seeking after reason. There is the chance for the audience to connect with its humanness – or not, as the case may be. They are invited to leave their ideological glasses behind and use their own eyes. The drama event aims to open an event out so that it can be examined in detail even though it lasts only a short time.

In the days of the plague, if one member of the family had the disease, the outside of the door was marked with a huge cross. The father blames the daughter for running down the street knocking on doors to look for her invisible friend. She has made the family social outcasts. The daughter is mad. Their house has been marked. It is a moment intended in accident time to open a *gap*, to rend a hole in the fabric of the situation, for the audience to enter and face the *invisible object* as described above.

The gap

The *gap* is an important part of Bond's theorizing. He argues that we live in the *gap* where we have the chance to explain ourselves to ourselves, to make meanings, but instead the world is interpreted for us by authority, by all those forces in society that claim to be able to explain what is actually open to exploration. The media, the church, politicians and other authority voices vie with each other, or combine together, to fill the *gap* with meaning. How to open it again is the role of the drama event.

The invisible object

The invisible object can be misleading as a term. It does not necessarily relate to an object but to the objective situation – what is objectively there rather than what is perceived in ideology. So far the play, the story of the play, has shown a family in apparently perilous circumstances, with a father doing his best to protect them and an obdurate girl bringing the whole family into danger. It brings to a head the clash of corrupted reason with imagination searching for humanness. This way of describing it loads the way the answer should come out, but for the children who have been following the story it is different. The daughter has been behaving apparently totally irrationally. The father, despite his authoritarian stance, has been trying to protect the family. She is mad and he is sane. So for the young audience it is a question for them of what they see and how they judge it. The *invisible object* is opened out only through enactment. It is where the actor as artist has to be at her most creative. It depends on the *way* the whole event is enacted, on *how* she goes limp, *how* the mother betrays her, *how* the father stands or sits to give his orders. The way such things are enacted will open the *gap* for the imagination to be called into action.

Bond and classroom drama

Many of the terms Bond uses may be unfamiliar in relation to classroom drama. This is true of the first encounter with all terms coined by dramatists and educators trying to develop form in drama. Heathcote's 'other', 'Mantle of the Expert', 'frame distance', 'teacher in role'; Bolton's 'second dimension of role', 'angle of connection'; Brecht's 'not-but', 'montage', '*gestus*'; Boal's 'spectactor', are all examples of terms that might well mystify on first hearing. However, they quickly become accepted terminology as their use is understood and practised. I predict it will be the same with Bond's terminology once it comes to be understood, practised and explored in the theatre and in process drama. This is already the case in Norway where as Kari Heggstad points out, 'Bond's concepts such as *centre* and *site* have become especially important in the devising and rehearsal stages of production' (Heggstad, 2013: 264).

To recapitulate some of the areas covered so far. In the earlier part of the book I took pains to point out the dearth of references to ideology in the many books on drama in education and how, in my view, this is a central weakness of these publications. Bond has recognized that it is no use using reason against reason. He has brought to centre stage the key role of imagination in relation to reason (see Bond, 1995b). Human value resides in the imagination, not in reason. Reason and imagination really cannot be separated. 'Reason and imagination should not be thought of as two tracks of a train-line – in life they cross over (and this is either revelatory or confusing) and drama attempts to control the exchange between the two' (Bond, 2013b). By opening out extreme moments for reflection without breaking the story, moments where questions of human value are at stake, the imagination is invited to set to work: to see beyond the apparent to the real. As in the Enlightenment, reasoning is imbued with human values, with the imagining of how life might be freer and more human. This is the central pursuit of Bondian drama.

It remains to start examining whether any of Bond's innovations in theatre form can help us take a step forward in classroom drama – a step nearer to a new theory of drama in education.

Notes

[1] The tenth, *The Angry Roads*, has been written but not yet performed.

[2] At first glance this may seem similar to O'Toole's diagram of drama elements, which has four contexts rather than sites: 'the real context – general purposes; the context of the setting – specific purposes; the context of the medium – the participant group; [and] inside the drama' (O'Toole, 1992: 6). This is a development of an earlier diagram in O'Toole and Haseman (1988) that appears without the outer contexts. However, this seems just to indicate that the drama would need to address the various dimensions of the contexts in which it was created, rather than these being embedded in the drama, influencing the purpose rather than the form and content of the drama. It is, in fact, quite different to Bond's sites.

[3] The National Theatre has also turned its back on Bond's latest plays. For example it refused the chance to premiere *Coffee* and *The Crime of the Twenty-first Century* (Bond, 2000: 1).

Chapter 8

Towards new components of classroom drama as art

Writing this seems presumptuous and over bold. Yet, I could not and would not have started this review of where we are in DiE if I did not have serious concerns about the state of drama in general: in mainstream theatre but also in classroom drama. On the other hand, I feel confident that I am on to something. I have had reasonably close contact with Bond over many years and have slowly come to understand more and more of his theory and practice. I know of no other person in the drama field who is more eager that we develop a drama that is humanly useful. I am lucky enough to receive, almost daily, a copy of some of the letters he writes to people around the world. They are constantly illuminating. Therefore, it is time to submit my own practice to examination in the light of Bond's writing. Strangely enough, it is *not* threatening, but, as I write this and it is not yet done, there is a sense of anticipation to see what will emerge. I have invited Chris Cooper to write the next section (pp. 154–64). It will be an analysis of the process drama on child abuse from a Bondian perspective.

Revisiting the process drama on child abuse
Chris Cooper

Davis's approach to process drama has been strongly influenced by DiE pioneers like Heathcote but even more by the work of Gavin Bolton. Since 1989 Davis has been the leading figure in bringing the work of Edward Bond to the attention of drama teachers and practitioners all over the world, with the aim of developing the art form of drama in education and process drama. Davis has introduced a new audience to Bond's analysis of the role of drama in society, its relationship to democracy and the foundation of the self through which we create our humanness (see Davis, 2005; Davis, 2009). It is clear that there are some areas of immediate convergence between Bond's approach to drama and Davis's approach in the child abuse process drama.

The key area of connection is that the participants in the process drama are not in a distanced relationship to the events but deeply immersed in the present. The process drama structure aims to engage them with 'being' in two worlds at the same time, or what Bolton refers to as *metaxis*. Bond aims to penetrate ideology by putting the audience inside the play or, as he describes it, by meeting themselves on the stage in order to experience and analyse the drama from within. The audience are involved in the drama but at key moments are confronted by drama events that demand reflection – without disengaging from the story – and that they reason imaginatively in order to reassess their values. Bond, like Bolton, works against the kind of distancing from the event in drama that is so prevalent in classroom drama today. However, Bond's notion of 'being' is central: we create our human being in the gap. In drama, the state of Radical Innocence we create as we enter into the world – the human imperative for justice – 'returns to confront its own corruption. It enters the maze of ideology and self-repression to create the logic of humanness. We are the dramatic species' (to repeat Bond, 2013e). This, I would argue, is also the aim of the process drama on child abuse. Given the space available one can do no more than make some general observations. But it would be useful to take each of the components of Bond's drama form and compare them to how Davis's process drama is working, so we can identify the connections between the two and see areas that have the potential for further development in a Bondian direction.

Story

As stated earlier, story is the way society understands itself and individuals understand themselves and is one of the key ways that individuals become encultured. The Bondian devices cannot be applied as a series of discrete tools or drama conventions, but interrelate as part of a holistic self-dramatizing process that is embedded in story. The use of story in Bond's plays is powerful and uninterrupted. It is out of story, the drama events embedded in the story, and the use of the extreme (see below), that the dramatic imperative is drawn from both the situation and the audience. The process drama builds towards a single major drama event: the arrival of the Child Support Officers (CSOs) to take the supposed abused child into care. There are two dimensions of story: the journey of the CSOs during the training to the main drama event at the end, and the case of the immigrant family. The immigrant family's story, however, is in reality subsumed into the story of the trainee CSOs. As in a Bond play, this story is not interrupted but interspersed with training sessions dealing with related concerns regarding child abuse. It seems to me, however, that the use of story is not as present or as strong in the process drama and therefore the dramatic imperative is not as immediate or accessible as in a Bondian play. This is not just a question of levels or modes of engagement (see Part Two) although this is important. Returning to *The Broken Bowl*, the human paradoxes of the situation and the characters (and therefore in the audience) built into the story are available or present much earlier for the audience or participant to make a relationship to. The extremity of the family's situation is immediately apparent but the situation is domestic and relates closely to the audience's lives. The structure of the play is such that the centre of the drama lies in the 'gap' between the daughter and her parents and the bowl she lays for her imaginary friend, the contents of the drama move into the gap and they will be imagined by the audience. In a Bond play there are often different narratives woven into the story that address central themes or concerns in the play and usually a central speech occurs early on that opens up the centre of the play, like the daughter's at the end of scene one in *The Broken Bowl* where she explains to her imaginary friend/self that it is dangerous outside and her father is afraid. The process drama uses story in a different way, to build the role, whereas in Bond it is used to build the situation, and to work for the equivalent in the process drama might require dealing with an image or enactment of an abuse case for example very early in the structure. This could then be present in some form throughout what follows right up to and including the decision to take the child from the parents.

Site

I think that it is true to say that all four Bondian sites are, to some extent, present in the process drama.

Site A, the social site, is strongly indicated through the new law that is to be implemented; the United Nations Conventions on the Rights of the Child; and the social context embodied by the teacher in shadow role and as the training officer. S/he continually mentions the need to implement the law and embodies the contradiction between law and justice that is at the heart of many social and political crises in the world and is also at the heart of the drama.

It is worth noting that *how* it is done is often what differentiates Bondian drama from conventional theatre. One can set out to enact but end up acting the play, or, in struggling to create a drama event, end up with an empty effect. A production of a Bond play can be, and often is, done without the understanding of what we are calling the Bondian approach. This creates poor productions. So in this instance *how* relates to the understanding of site in practice. The same must be said of the use of TiR (or any drama convention) in process drama. If the training officer is overzealous, the role is two dimensional and the signing reductive, even manipulative, and this closes down meaning and therefore denies full access to the site.

Site B, the specific sites of the drama, is strongly present as the newly enrolled trainees build their office workstations, the noticeboards and so on. They are also building themselves into role. This is different to the way it works with Bond. In presenting a play to the audience, Site B, in its design and the atmosphere created, is clearly particularizing the specific social context for the audience. In process drama the participants have to design and build the social context and, through this activity, build their own role engagement with the drama and create their own story. The story in a Bond play already exists. It is a given; we experience it in the specific sites as the story is enacted, and analyse its meaning from within. In this process drama the participants are creating the specific sites in order to build the role. The story is also a given, otherwise there would be no climax to the drama that everything builds towards, so the space for creating the story lies directly in relation to building the role; the attitudes and values of the CSOs in the specific sites. To extend the use of Site B in a more Bondian manner in the process drama, it might be possible to develop the existing tasks but to add new dimensions. For example, before asking the participants to share one personal thing each over tea and coffee, something that happened while in the car park or shopping and so on, they might be asked to think about a recent incident that occurred between them and their child that they would rather not share openly at this stage. They could perhaps write it down on a post-it note but keep it private, something that exposes the contradiction between justice and law. With this internalized, they could be invited to share the everyday incident with their colleague. If participants are not all parents there will be other angles of connection, such as a moment when they have broken the law – shoplifted, or stolen from someone and so on.

Site C conveys Sites A and B to the audience. Conversely it also conveys the audience to Sites A and B. In a Bond play, this is through the way it is enacted, the *how* again: the way everything in the play comes from the centre; the way objects are cathected and de-cathected; the way drama events are opened up in extreme situations to 'wreck the structures of ideology by exposing their presence in society and confronting them with the self' (Bond, 2013c); the invitation to the audience to activate their being, their imagination, their Radical Innocence in the gap that is there for them to enter. In the process drama the participants *are* Site C. They make it happen to themselves until it is happening and they are conscious of what is happening. They are the centre embodied: the central actions, images, and the text of their own drama. It depends on the success of the activities chosen: the filling in of the application form; the memories stirred up by the work in which they are engaged; the plays within the play of deciding what would count as a breach of the law in the new regime. All these build the connection and the immersion leading to the main event. The cathecting and de-cathecting of objects, however, is absent from the structure. All good drama teachers understand the significance of objects (the importance of their authenticity) in drama, but in Bondian drama this is arguably a dimension that is unique. Enactment in a Bond play is very close to 'being' in role. It is my belief that enacting a Drama Event (in or out of role) using the cathexis of objects lends a profundity and intensity to the level of engagement that not only mirrors that of being in role but also adds a different dimension in the gaps created between the enactor and the objects. This has the potential to take both the enactor and audience out of ideology and into the unknown precisely because the focus is on the objects being cathected. Bond responded to the exercise Davis introduces on tying shoelaces in Part Two by writing that:

> The child must tie the shoelaces before she can go to the shop with her mother. But why should she go to the shop with her mother? … The action is about a waiting mother and a working child. But they and the shoelaces seem to be bound together – not by a shoelace but by a chain, because it is ideological. In ideology the obligation has precedence over the object. (However, you can re-cathect the object.)

> … the child learns that the world is not made up of only her, the shoes and the laces. The child learns about chains. The chains are social. If (above) there is a situation of chains, the mother is using them. And she is being used by them – because the supermarket is doing to the mother what the mother is doing to the child. The supermarket is rattling its chains. How does rattling chains differ from tying shoelaces or tying parcels? Are chains only on slaves' ankles or are the child's hands chained?

> The exercise demonstrates the difference between self and site. Between self and society. Between natural law and self-and-society.
>
> (Bond, 2013b)

Through cathecting the object, the meaning or the reality of the situation has precedence over the object, rather than what ideology tells us is the situation.. Depending on how the moment is enacted, this holds the potential to reveal what Bond calls the Invisible Object, whereby the self-spectator, through a form of non-ideologized *metaxis*, is liberated. It seems to me that the potential to release this creativity within the site of the drama deepens the contradiction within the self in role. For example, at the climax of the process drama the girl could be clinging to an object that resonated and re-cathected the objects they have been working with in building the role.

Site D is the audience as site of imagination. This involves the audience entering the gap in the drama events. The participants in the process drama may be on the edge of Site D when they are judging the short drama scenes they have created: the three short scenes to go in a training video in order to find the line between what is acceptable punishment of children and what is not. These short scenes, however, could not really be classed as drama events. They are created in ideology and likely to be viewed in ideology even though the imagination has been activated, unless there is a cathected object at the centre of them. The main parallel to Bond's drama events to be found in the process drama is the moment when they go to take the child into care and meet a child with cerebral palsy. They are not prepared for this and the certainty of the steps they are taking suddenly disappears and, depending on how this is enacted, they are left floundering. How they respond in that moment will be more or less human. The same can happen for the other CSOs watching the event on live video who will potentially experience what Bond calls accident time.

Centre

Like all good drama, the process drama clearly has a centre. This is held in exploring the problem of solving social needs through law enforcement. However, each activity in the process drama does not have the centre reflected in the task. The tasks: filling in the application form; making the workspace; creating notices for the noticeboard; having a chat with a colleague; writing down a memory; making three scenes for the training video; sorting the contents of the envelope; and publicly signing for or against action, are all important because they protect the participants into role. The main event of collecting the child is different because it is here that the centre of the drama (the state, family and the relationship between justice and law) is at its most explicit and is dramatized. There could be further opportunities to build the centre more explicitly into most if not all of the tasks. For example, could there have been a space on the application form requiring them to answer whether or not they think the law should act to defend abused children, and to ask what sort of powers the law enforcers should be entitled to? There could be more external social pressures (Site A) introduced into their training such as press coverage that they had to process for example. If Bondian drama is to work the centre is inseparable from the site; you cannot have one without the other. The centre is contained in all of the sites and specifically located in Site C because here we are in the process of conveying or accessing Sites A and B to Site D and vice versa and this will relate very much to how the situation is enacted, the images created, the objects cathected and so on. The Bondian concept of the centre and how it is used is an important area for development in process drama.

Enactment

To repeat, enactment in a Bond play is very close to 'being' in role, which means that the enacting needs to resonate the main concerns of the drama. Certainly the building into role in the process drama did not proceed from Stanislavskian concerns with psychological imperatives but did try to build a relationship between the needs of the role and the participant creating the role: the social in the personal and the personal in the social. If the centre had been more strongly present in each of the activities it would have helped focus the personal dimension onto the social purpose of the role. This would have kept the potential contradictions in the actions of the role more under consideration.

Drama creates situations that break the structures of ideology and exposes their presence in society by confronting the audience with the extreme so that the self is returned to its original state of innocence and creativity. When this is so, the ideological structures are penetrated by using the imagination, not imagination as occupied by ideology, which is part of the self and the objective social situation. In drama we can create situations that lay bare this connection. In a Bond play these situations are inhabited by the actors and this leads to enactment and the invisible object; the enactment of humanness. Young people who are much more able than adults to step into 'being' in role are closer to the use of imagination but lack the technical skill of the actor. To achieve enactment in a drama event therefore requires carefully structured tasks, and time (repeatedly working on the moment under guidance usually), that enables the participants to stay in the Site and closer to the Centre. For example, referring back to the task of relating a domestic incident between CSOs over coffee, it would be possible to construct an incident (using water in plastic cups) when, during the telling of this apparently straightforward event of the night before, the coffee is spilt across the table by the one telling the story to her colleague. There is an infinite variety of ways that this could happen and how the other colleague might react. Is it a result of an unexpected shaking hand, a surprisingly sudden movement, a thump of a hand on the table? With the right teacher interventions, the spilling of the coffee slows down time and opens up the logic of the situation for participants. What has happened here? As an event it can take us to the extreme and has the potential to take us to the centre of the drama which, as Bond says, lies in the 'gap' between the teller of the anecdote, the spilled coffee and her colleague. The meaning of the contradiction between what is being said and being done will move into the gap and they will be imagined by the enactors and any audience if shared within the group, potentially revealing layers of meaning that the enactors are unaware of. There are other dimensions to build out from: Who reacts to the spilt coffee first? How do they attempt to protect the important papers the coffee is spilling across the surface of the table towards and so on. This could be explored in pairs guided by the teacher. This then is another area for closer examination.

Cathexis (mainly of objects)

Cathexis is almost entirely missing from the use of the sites in the process drama. For example, just as the use of the bowl in *The Broken Bowl* journeys through Bond's play, objects could be used throughout the child abuse drama to get behind ideology. To go back to Bond's example of the tying of the shoelaces exercise for example, shoes and shoelaces could be a recurring object introduced by the teacher or TiR into the tasks. Built into the climax of the drama might be the insistence of the Mother on putting on the girl's shoes, and this might be disputed by either the girl or the father or the CSOs; or the girl might want her favourite shoes; the Mother might throw them at the CSOs and so on. The shoes could become the conduit for all the energy flowing from the conflict at the centre of the drama, and this will reveal much more than improvisation based on talking or argument. Before this point the teacher might have to ask each group to include an object in their scenes that appeared as creative and destructive at different points. Clearly, there needs to be further exploration of the ways in which cathexis can develop the process drama.

Extreme

The extreme seems to be present at least in the final event of the drama but there would surely be value in building in the extreme earlier in tasks leading up to it. The extreme is critical to Bondian drama and getting behind ideology. It does not have to be violent, it can be comic. It enables us to see beyond convention in a new or different way. Fairy tales use the extreme all the time to engage self-creativity. For example *Hansel and Gretel* begins with a famine and the children overhearing their stepmother demanding that their father abandon them in the forest.

Drama event (with accident time, the gap and the invisible object)

The final moment seems to be the clearest drama event. It opens a space in the story for analysis and the imagination to set to work. Remember the response reported by one of the participants quoted earlier: 'I thought on the one hand as a mother and having a child and on the other as a child protection officer and in both roles thinking, how should I protect her? Has anyone the right to decide for me or for her what is better for us? Could I refuse and stand face to face towards the law? Taking her could be helpful or painful to me and her …' This seems like accident time at work: a gap has opened up where the participant is wondering about the child and her future, herself as a mother, and struggling with the contradiction between justice and the law, where imagination is leading reason. This seems likely to be in Site D.

The invisible object in Bond's plays depends on how the whole play is constructed and creatively enacted to make the objective situation apparent. In the theatre this requires the best sort of creativity from the actor, but experience tells me that it is possible to create it in the moment of participant creating/experiencing the situation in process drama. *Metaxis* means we are not only in the role in the situation ourselves but that we are aware of what we are doing. Earlier Davis mentioned being conscious of the psychological present when working with another in process drama. This relates to how a moment is enacted or a word or phrase spoken. This is a significant area for further exploration because it demands that we attend to how we respond both in or out of role, within or without ideology. In Bond's plays audiences are free to respond because there is no wrong answer, and the more the audience is engaged the more they will understand about how people get into situations and deeds that make them more human or less. The same needs to be present in process drama. The recollections of the Palestinian participants to being in the moment of taking the girl from the family reveal a powerful emotional connection to the situation and self-awareness from within. They are shocked by their own situation. The process drama is structured to this end; the CSOs have been taken in (or in a few cases not) by ideology and acted against the human interest of themselves and others. This is useful, but is what is structured enough for those watching to take them out of ideology: to understand themselves in the social situation? A detailed analysis of the mechanics of what and how this was enacted would be necessary before we could see in what way the drama event was occurring for those watching it and how the drama devices could be further deployed in order to create accident time.

Summary

The key area of connection between Bondian drama and this process drama is that the participants are not in a distanced relationship to the events but deeply immersed in the present, or what Bolton refers to as *metaxis*. Bond, like Bolton, works against distancing from the event in drama.

There are also significant differences, or differences of degree, which relate not only to what is done but *how* it is done in the shared aim to dislodge ideology's spectacles. This process drama uses story in a different way, to build the role, whereas in Bond it is used to build the situation. I think that all four Bondian sites are to some extent present in the process drama. The strongest connection between the child abuse drama and the Bondian site, in my opinion, lies in the use of Site A, the social sites. Site B is also very present but, as with story, the emphasis in building Site B in the process drama is very much directed towards building the role rather than building the situation. The area least developed in the process drama is Site C, which is the site most concerned with unsettling ideology's spectacles, because it is here in Bond that through enactment the audience enters accident time and in the gap created by drama events the invisible object can also be created.

In my experience of working on Bond's plays, I have found that while image and action and the separation of what you see and hear is extremely significant, the cathecting, re-cathecting and de-cathecting of objects and space, including rooms, is absolutely critical. It is how the centre becomes tangible for Site D, which, as the audience as site of imagination, involves them entering the gap to make meaning in the event to confront ideology with the self. We noted that Site D seems to be present in the final task of the CSOs going to take the girl from the parents. But it is not clear if there has been enough access to Site C leading up to this moment for those watching to enter accident time. There is also another consideration: leading up to the climax of the drama, has there been enough access to the holism of Site C present for those enacting it to really exploit the potential that moment holds to unsettle their ideological spectacles? This relates to the absence of the centre in some of the framing tasks in the process drama. As Bond succinctly defines it himself, 'Usually it's [the centre] the specific event or situation on which the story is based. But reality is holistic and the centre is found in every part of the drama. So everything in the play and its performance – writing, designing, direction, acting – must pass through the centre. Otherwise there is theatre instead of drama' (Bond, 2013f).

If the centre had been more strongly present in each of the activities, this would have helped focus the personal dimension onto the social purpose of the role. It would have made the potential contradictions of the role (the tensions between the state and the family and law and justice) more extreme. This is certainly present in the final event of the drama. But I believe there would be value in exploring the potential for seeking to access the extreme earlier, in tasks building up to the final event so as to engage Site D, by working for drama events.

The main danger in any drama, and one that I believe Bond manages to avoid in his plays, is that the students in the process drama create the 'play', enter it, experience it and reflect on it, still with their ideology spectacles on. The event at the climax of the process drama had a significant impact on those enacting it and has similarities to the impact of a Bondian drama event but there has been no clear pathway to unsettling the gaze of ideology leading up to it. How the Bondian devices that I have analysed in relation to the process drama can assist in this unsettling of the ideological spectacles would be the area for further examination and testing.

Response to Chris Cooper's analysis

Cooper's analysis points to a way forward. He identifies the key experience in the drama as the moment the CSOs arrive to take the child into custody. There certainly seems to have been an unsettling of how those CSOs thought the world should operate as they suddenly found themselves acting 'against the human interest of themselves and others', as Cooper puts it. For the participants in this culminating drama event, the CSOs and the child's carers, there has clearly been this entering into a gap where, temporarily, they have lost their ideological bearings. But, as Cooper points out, we have no way of knowing how far those watching, as a sort of audience, were entering accident time or even what was happening for them. This points to the importance of those dimensions of a Bondian approach that were missing from the drama: the absence of story running through all the activities; the centre not being made available in all the role-building activities; the lack of drama events earlier in the drama; the lack of the use of cathected objects that could be de-cathected and re-cathected; the danger of two dimensional role-playing of the TiR; and, I would add, a big question mark over whether or not the participants were being over-manipulated into the final event. It was precisely my intention to replicate the steady way in which ideology seeps into our daily lives unnoticed and takes us over, so that we end up shouting at school students for talking too loudly in the corridors. But whether or not the CSOs needed more space to challenge their steady manipulation remains as a question for me. All this points to the importance of exploring how Site C is approached in process drama.

So there are more questions than answers and those whose interest has been caught by the arguments put forward in this book will now have to experiment and seek the answers through their practice. I recognize that I have made only the smallest of steps towards a new theory of drama in education. However, taking it further would need another book. I look forward to reading it – or will I be tempted to try to write it?

Conclusion

In this book I have attempted to set out the dangerous social context, worldwide, that we have entered. To repeat a quotation from the beginning of the book, I argued that we live in a world where:

> Something is profoundly wrong with the way we live today. For thirty years we have made a virtue out of the pursuit of material self-interest: indeed, this very pursuit now constitutes whatever remains of our sense of collective purpose. We know what things cost but have no idea what they are worth. We no longer ask of a judicial ruling or a legislative act: Is it good? Is it fair? Is it right? Will it bring about a better society or a better world? Those used to be *the* political questions, even if they invited no easy answers. We must learn once again to pose them.
>
> (Judt, 2010: 1–2)

Or as Bond puts it, 'We are in the third of the crises in which a new form of consciousness must be created so that society can function and still be human' (Bond, 2013a: 13). I have argued that there is a crisis in classroom drama where we are standing still or even going into reverse and pursuing outdated forms of drama that cannot meet the needs of young people today. The main drama approaches we are using cannot help them create that new form of consciousness needed for a human society. At the centre of the problem is the lack of attention to the nature of ideology and how to undermine it. During the Enlightenment, reason was led by a humanizing imagination. Now, reason is led by a corrupt ideology that starts and finishes with the pursuit of money and profit.

We are headed for a future that is opened up in all of Bond's later plays: *Coffee*; *The Crime of the Twenty-first Century*; *Born*; *People*; *Innocence*; and these concerns are also echoed in all the Big Brum plays. They are even reflected in popular teenage fiction such as *The Hunger Games* and in popular science-fiction films like *Elysium*. What is missing from these popular representations of this grim future is a means to enable a humanizing imagination to set to work. The same is true of our classroom drama. It remains trapped in distancing modes influenced by an outdated Brechtian practice that remains within ideology and uses reasoning from within that framework. Bond's drama form provides a rich resource from which classroom drama teachers can examine and develop their practice: to help young people imagine the real.

In one of Bond's emails in response to a draft of this book, he picked out the little incident of the girl tying her shoelaces to which Cooper also refers. One short part of his reflection puts the whole book into perspective. The girl is intent on tying her shoelace and the mother has to get them both to the shops to buy the bargains. I described the child's investment as 'I want to be grown up', but Bond points out that it could have been 'I want to grow up'. And as he goes on to point out, 'These are the opposites of Ideology and Creativity'. The child might choose to starve rather than submit to the ideological chains that are pulling her mother towards the door. This would mark out the child's struggle to be a human being. Such a view could lead into a revision and rethinking of the 'model' level in the five layers of meaning and all the other levels in that useful tool: an indication of just one of the routes for developing the theory and practice of making drama.

Edward Bond is one of the world's leading playwrights. He has already joined forces with theatre in education. This book aims to open a door onto his work but it also invites him into the drama classroom to work with us there.

Early on in the book I quoted Gavin Bolton about one of his long-term aims, namely to set up drama that helps young people decide when and when not to adapt to society's norms (page 22). I end the book by acknowledging the key role Bolton has played in developing drama in education. He is the drama education practitioner I have been most influenced by in my teaching life. His influence has brought me closer to a Bondian drama form. Heathcote was undoubtedly the great creator and inventor of drama devices and drama forms; however it may be time to see that Bolton, in continuing to develop Heathcote's early work on the 'living through' experience in new directions, chose a more *useful* path for drama to take. I know that Bolton will strongly disagree with this statement but it does mark out the perspective I have outlined in this book; it is a statement that I know will be controversial but one I need to make.

Afterword

David Davis has written a stimulating and challenging book. The sense of conviction is strong and the rhetoric is powerful. The aim of providing a new theory of drama in education is also ambitious. Even so, the book does not end on a note of triumphant closure but rather sets an agenda for further writing and research. By building on Gavin Bolton's concept of 'making' drama and by drawing on Edward Bond's theory and practice, the book has provided the drama teaching world with a much needed provocation to thought and action.

As the book demonstrates, the 'living through' approach recommended here became marginalized in drama teaching. This happened for a number of reasons. The separation between drama and theatre gave way to a more inclusive approach that sought to rehabilitate theatre. 'Living through' drama, because of its perceived distance from notions of rehearsal, acting and performing, sat less comfortably with the new, inclusive approach. It is very telling therefore that David Davis has drawn on a theatre theorist and practitioner to extend the theoretical underpinning and create links that have not been previously recognized. After the healing of theatre/drama divisions, a view arose that everything that goes on in drama teaching can be described as both 'drama' and 'theatre'. This avoids the absurd division that had developed in previous years but lacks the necessary nuance that asks what kind of theatre, what kind of drama is appropriate and necessary for the times in which we live? Not all readers will necessarily agree with the answer provided in this book but it is important that the question has been asked.

A second reason for the decline of a 'living through' approach was simply the practical challenge of making this style of drama achieve success regularly in the classroom, particularly with the pre-adolescent age group. The conventions approach made process drama teaching less rarefied and more accessible. It is therefore valuable to see such a variety of practical examples and guidance for teachers in this book. Chris Cooper's analysis of the child abuse drama and David Davis's own reflective comments make this a particularly fascinating and informative read, where art and pedagogy come together so well. Newcomers to this way of working may be surprised at the slow build-up in the sessions but this kind of investment in the work is essential for success. Achieving the necessary balance between teacher direction and pupil engagement requires considerable skill.

A third reason for the neglect of 'living through' drama was theoretical. The emphasis on 'being in the event' rather than 'pretending', on direct rather than distanced involvement, on feeling rather than cognition pointed inwards, making it hard to distinguish authentic experience from deceit or self-deception. This is not just a question of formal assessment in schools, but if concrete evidence remains elusive this makes the approach vulnerable to criticism. The use of Bond's notion of 'enactment' that seeks to 'resonate' the chosen themes rather than display skill in acting is helpful here because it focuses on what is observable. Similarly, in David Davis's account of the key components of a drama event the word 'feeling' is not used but the focus is more on the external dimensions. Even so, I think there is more work to be done in distinguishing the reflection that is acknowledged as being part of *metaxis* in living through drama from the reflection that is part of more distanced modes of working.

It is a central feature of the argument, of course, that the nature of the engagement in drama cannot be separated from considerations of content; the concept of ideology is therefore central to the theory. A small minority of readers may not see drama and education as being political in any way; for them this book will make little sense. However the vast majority of drama writers and practitioners who believe in the importance of criticality and are attracted to theories of critical pedagogy will I suspect be sympathetic to the analysis of the current social context. Where they may differ is with regard to the implications for drama practice. This book presents a challenge and, through its criticism of the work of a range of writers, an implicit invitation to dialogue. The hope is that the drama education world will take up the challenge and engage in the debate.

Gavin Bolton is an important figure in this book and is widely respected in the world of drama education. His impact has been huge, but he has himself tended to downplay his own contribution to the field particularly in relation to the influence of Dorothy Heathcote. David Davis is right to give him the proper recognition that he deserves. Central to much of Bolton's writing was his concern that different ways of engaging in drama/theatre offer different qualities of experience that have profound implications for learning and pedagogy. This idea is also central to this book and would be a good starting point for the debate that must surely follow its publication.

Mike Fleming

Appendix

	Delete role not taken where there is a choice	Level of emotion	Feeling predominant (not conscious of thought process)	Feeling thoughtfully	Thinking feelingly	Rational thought
1	In-role as residents					
2	Care workers					
3	Care workers before committee					
	As care workers					
	As committee					
4	Out of role					
5	Lecture/demo					
	As demonstrators					
	As audience of trainees					
6	Scene from play					
	As performers					
	As audience					

Figure A.1: Full chart to capture level and form of student engagement

References

Abbott, L. (2011) 'Mantle of the expert: Palestine 2010'. *The Journal for Drama in Education*, 27 (1), 14–24.

— (2013) 'Mantle of the Expert.com'. Online. www.mantleoftheexpert.com/articles/history-lessons-regarding-mantleoftheexpert-com/ (accessed 19 July 2013).

Amoiropoulos, K. (2013) 'Balancing Gaps: An investigation of Edward Bond's theory and practice for drama'. PhD thesis, Birmingham City University.

Anderson, M. (2012) *Master Class in Drama Education: Transforming teaching and learning*. London: Continuum.

Barenboim, D. (2012) Interviewed on BBC Two, 28 July 2012.

Best, D. (1992) *The Rationality of Feeling: Understanding the arts in education*. London: Falmer Press.

Bettelheim, B. (1976) *The Uses of Enchantment: The meaning and importance of fairy tales*. New York: Alfred A. Knopf.

Blatner, A. (ed.) with Wiener, D.J. (2007) *Interactive and Improvisational Drama: Varieties of applied theatre and performance*. New York: Universe, Inc.

Boal, A. (1995) *The Rainbow of Desire: The Boal method of theatre and therapy*. London: Routledge.

Bolton, G. (1976) 'Drama teaching – A personal statement'. *Insight, Journal of the British Children's Theatre Association*, Summer.

— (1979) *Towards a Theory of Drama in Education*. London: Longman.

— (1984) *Drama as Education*. London: Longman.

— (1986) 'Emotion in the dramatic process: Is it an adjective or a verb?'. In Bolton, G., Davis, D., and Lawrence, C. (eds) *Gavin Bolton: Selected writings on drama in education*. London: Longman.

— (1992) *New Perspectives on Classroom Drama*. London: Simon and Schuster Education.

— (1998) *Acting in Classroom Drama: A critical analysis*. Stoke-on-Trent: Trentham Books.

— (2010a) 'Drama in education: Learning medium or arts process'. In Davis, D. (ed.) *Gavin Bolton: Essential writings*. Stoke-on-Trent: Trentham Books.

— (2010b) 'Re-interpretations of Heathcote's "living through" drama'. In Davis, D. (ed.) *Gavin Bolton: Essential writings*. Stoke-on-Trent: Trentham Books.

— (2010c) 'Towards a conceptual framework for classroom acting behaviour'. In Davis, D. (ed.) *Gavin Bolton: Essential writings*. Stoke-on-Trent: Trentham Books.

Bond, E. (1995a) *Coffee*. London: Methuen.

— (1995b) 'Notes on imagination'. In Bond, E. *Coffee*. London: Methuen.

— (2000) *The Hidden Plot*. London: Methuen.

— (2004) Unpublished letter to unidentified student.

— (2009) 'Foreword'. In Nicholson, H. *Theatre and Education*. Basingstoke: Palgrave Macmillan.

— (2012a) *Bochum Talk Re-constructed*. Unpublished paper. Available online as 'The third crisis: The state of future drama' at www.edwardbond.org/Comment/comment.html (accessed 16 April 2014).

— (2012b) *A Short and Troubled Essay on Being Human*. Unpublished.

— (2013a) 'The first word'. *The Journal for Drama in Education*, 29 (1) Spring, 31–8.

— (2013b) Personal letter to the author, unpublished.

— (2013c) Personal letter to the author, unpublished.

— (2013d) Letter to Big Brum TIE, unpublished.

— (2013e) Personal letter to the author, unpublished.

— (2013f) Letter to Razzaq Zghair Shnawa, unpublished.

Bowell, P., and Heap, B.S. (2001) *Planning Process Drama*. London: David Fulton Publishers.

Braverman, D. (2002) *Playing a Part: Drama and citizenship*. Stoke-on-Trent: Trentham Books.

Brecht, B. (1978) *Brecht on Theatre: The development of an aesthetic*. Trans. and ed. Willett, J. Originally 1964. London: Eyre Methuen.

Bruner, J.S. (1974) *Beyond the Information Given*. London: Allen & Unwin.

— (1986) *Actual Minds, Possible Worlds*. London: Harvard University Press.

— (1996) *The Culture of Education*. London: Harvard University Press.

Carroll, J., Anderson, M., and Cameron, D. (2006) *Real Players? Drama, technology and education*. Stoke-on-Trent: Trentham Books.

Chinyowa, K. (2007) 'Frames of metacommunication: Examples from African theatre for development'. *NJ: Drama Australia Journal*, 31 (1), 33–43.

Chomsky, N. (2011) *Hope and Prospects*. London: Penguin.

Cohen-Cruz, J., and Schutzman, M. (eds) (2005) *A Boal Companion: Dialogues on theatre and cultural politics*. London: Routledge.

Cooper, C. (2013) 'The Performer in TIE'. In Jackson, A., and Vine, C. (eds) *Learning Through Theatre: The changing face of theatre in education*. London: Routledge.

Coventon, J. (ed.) (2011) *Drama to Inspire: A London Drama Guide to excellent practice in drama for young people*. Stoke-on-Trent: Trentham Books.

Cuthbertson, L. (2011) 'Throw your mistempered weapons to the ground'. In Coventon, J. (ed.) *Drama to Inspire: a London Drama Guide to excellent practice in drama for young people*. Stoke-on-Trent: Trentham Books.

Damasio, A. (2003) *Looking for Spinoza: Joy, sorrow and the feeling brain*. London: Harcourt.

Damrosch, L. (2007) *Jean-Jacques Rousseau: Restless genius*. Boston: Houghton Mifflin.

Davis, D. (ed.) (2005) *Edward Bond and the Dramatic Child*. Stoke-on-Trent: Trentham Books.

— (2007) 'Edward Bond and drama in education'. In Rasmussen, B. (ed.) *Drama Boreale*. Trondheim: Tapir Akademisk Forlag.

— (2009) 'Introduction'. In Bond, E. *Saved: Student edition*. London: Methuen.

— (ed.) (2010) *Gavin Bolton: Essential writings*. Stoke-on-Trent: Trentham Books.

Dickenson, R., and Neelands, J. (2006) *Improving Your Primary School Through Drama*. London: David Fulton Publishers.

Doona, J. (2013a) *Drama Lessons for the Primary School Year: Calendar-Based learning activities*. London: Routledge.

— (2013b) *Secondary Drama: A creative source book: Practical inspiration for teachers*. London: Routledge.

Eagleton, T. (2007) *Ideology: An introduction*. 2nd ed. London: Verso.

Economist Intelligence Unit (2012) *The Learning Curve: Lessons in country performance in education*. London: Pearson.

Eriksson, S. (2011) 'Distancing'. In Schonmann, S. (ed.) *Key Concepts in Theatre/ Drama Education*. Rotterdam: Sense Publishers.

Farmer, D. (2011) *Learning Through Drama in the Primary Years*. Norwich: Drama Resource.

Fautley, M., Hatcher, R., and Millard, E. (2011) *Remaking the Curriculum: Re-engaging young people in secondary school*. Stoke-on-Trent: Trentham Books.

Financial Times Lexicon of economic terms. Online. http://lexicon.ft.com/ Term?term=globalisation (accessed 10 February 2013).

Fleming, M. (2001) *Teaching Drama in Primary and Secondary Schools: An integrated approach*. London: David Fulton Publishers.

— (2011) *Starting Drama Teaching*. 3rd ed. London: Routledge.

Franken, A. (2003) *Lies and the Lying Liars Who Tell Them: A fair and balanced look at the right*. London: Penguin.

Freedland, J. (2012) 'Labour has to voice this anger before it's too late'. *Guardian*, 7 July.

Gee, M. (2011) 'The contribution of drama'. In Fautley, M., Hatcher, R., and Millard, E. *Remaking the Curriculum: Re-engaging young people in secondary school*. Stoke-on-Trent: Trentham Books.

Gillham, G. (1974) *Condercum School Report for Newcastle upon Tyne Local Education Authority* (unpublished).

— (1988) 'What life is for: An analysis of Dorothy Heathcote's "levels" of explanation'. *Theatre and Education Journal*, 1, 31–9.

— (1997) 'What life is for: An analysis of Dorothy Heathcote's "levels" of explanation'. *SCYPT Journal*, 34, 9–17.

Goffman, E. (1974) *Frame Analysis: An essay on the organization of experience*. New York: Harper and Row.

Gove, M. (2012) 'Education Secretary Michael Gove speaks at the Independent Academies Association'. Online. www.education.gov.uk/inthenews/speeches/ a00217008/secretary-of-state-gives-speech-to-iaa- (accessed 13 February 2013).

Greenfield, S. (2009) 'Is the web changing our brains?' Online. www.bbc.co.uk/ blogs/digitalrevolution/2009/09/susan-greenfield-is-the-web-ch.shtml (accessed 18 October 2013).

Hatcher, R. (2011) 'Liberating the supply side, managing the market'. In Hatcher, R., and Jones, K. (eds) *No Country for the Young*. London: Tufnell Press.

Hawkes, D. (2003) *Ideology*. 2nd ed. London: Routledge.

Heathcote, D. (1984a) 'Material for significance'. In Johnson, L., and O'Neill, C. (eds) *Dorothy Heathcote: Collected writings on education and drama*. London: Hutchinson.

— (1984b) 'Signs and portents'. In Johnson, L., and O'Neill, C. (eds) *Dorothy Heathcote: Collected writings on education and drama*. London: Hutchinson.

Heathcote, D., and Bolton, G. (1995) *Drama for Learning: Dorothy Heathcote's mantle of the expert approach to education*. Portsmouth, NH: Heinemann.

Heathcote, D., and Fiala, O. (1980) 'Preparing Teachers to Use Drama: The Caucasian Chalk Circle'. In Heathcote, D. *Drama as Context*. Sheffield: NATE Publications.

Hegel, G.W.F. (1955) *Lectures on the History of Philosophy*, vol. 3. Trans. Haldane, E.S., and Simson, F.H. London: Routledge and Kegan Paul.

Heggstad, K. (2013) 'Norway and the Nordic countries'. In Jackson, A., and Vine, C. (eds) *Learning Through Theatre: The changing face of theatre in education*. London: Routledge.

Hessell, S. (2011) *Time for Outrage*. London: Quartet Books.

Hickmann, L., and Alexander, T. (eds) (1998) *The Essential Dewey Vol. 1: Pragmatism, Education, Democracy*. Bloomington: Indiana University Press.

Hirrt, N. (2011) 'Competencies, polarisation, flexibility: European education policy in the era of economic crisis'. In Hatcher, R., and Jones, K. (eds), *No Country for the Young*. London: The Tufnell Press.

Hornbrook, D. (1989) *Education and Dramatic Art*. Oxford: Blackwell.

Hughes, R. (2003) *Goya*. London: Harvill.

Hutton, W. (2012) 'Bank rate-fixing scandals reveal the rotten heart of capitalism'. *Observer*, 23 December.

Israel, J. (2010) *A Revolution of the Mind: Radical enlightenment and the intellectual origins of modern democracy*. Oxford and Princeton, NJ: Princeton University Press.

Jackson, A., and Vine, C. (eds) (2013) *Learning Through Theatre: The changing face of theatre in education*. London: Routledge.

Judt, T. (2010) *Ill Fares the Land*. London: Penguin.

Jürs-Munby, K. (2006) 'Introduction'. In Lehmann, H.T. (ed.) *Postdramatic Theatre*. London: Routledge.

Kant, I. (2009) *An Answer to the Question: What is enlightenment?* London: Penguin.

Katafiasz, K. (2005) 'Alienation is the theatre of Auschwitz'. In Davis, D. (ed.) *Edward Bond and the Dramatic Child*. Stoke-on-Trent: Trentham Books.

Kempe, A., and Nicholson, H. (2007) *Learning to Teach Drama 11–18*. 2nd ed. London: Continuum.

Klein, N. (2007) *The Shock Doctrine: The rise of disaster capitalism*. Toronto: Knopf Canada.

Lanchester, J. (2010) *Whoops! Why everyone owes everyone and no one can pay*. London: Penguin.

Lehmann, H.-T. (2006) *Postdramatic Theatre*. London: Routledge.

Lewis, M., and Rainer, J. (2012) *Teaching Classroom Drama and Theatre: Practical projects for secondary schools* (Revised edition). London: Routledge.

Linds, W. (2005) '*Metaxis*: Dancing (in) the in-between'. In Cohen-Cruz, J., and Schutzman, M. (eds) *A Boal Companion: Dialogues on theatre and cultural politics*. London: Routledge.

Marks, D. (2011) *Thomas Paine: Complete works and biography ultimate edition*. Everlasting Flames Publishing.

Massey, D. (2005) *For Space*. London: Sage Publications.

Masson, J. (1990) *Against Therapy: Emotional tyranny and the myth of psychological healing*. London: Fontana.

MERIP (Middle East Research and Information Project) www.merip.org/palestine-israel_primer/occupied-terr-jeru-pal-isr.html (accessed 19 July 2013).

Migration Policy Institute Data Hub, www.migrationinformation.org/datahub/wmm.cfm (accessed 10 February 2013).

Milne, S. (2012) *The Revenge of History: The battle for the 21st century*. London: Verso.

— (2013a) 'There is a problem with welfare, but it's not "shirkers"'. *Guardian*, 9 January.

— (2013b) 'Think there's no alternative? Latin America has a few'. *Guardian*, 20 February, 26.

Monbiot, G. (2000) *Captive State: The corporate takeover of Britain*. Basingstoke: Macmillan.

— (2012) 'A rightwing insurrection is usurping our democracy'. *Guardian*, 1 October.

Morris, P. (ed.) (1994) *The Bakhtin Reader*. London: Edward Arnold.

Muir, A. (1996) *New Beginnings: Knowledge and form in the drama of Bertolt Brecht and Dorothy Heathcote*. Stoke-on-Trent: Trentham Books and Birmingham: University of Central England.

Nadler, S. (1999) *Spinoza: A life*. Cambridge: Cambridge University Press.

Neelands, J. (1984) *Making Sense of Drama*. London: Heinemann Educational Books.

— (1990) *Structuring Drama Work*. Cambridge: Cambridge University Press.

— (1992) 'Learning through imagined experience'. In O'Connor, P. (ed.) (2010) *Creating Democratic Citizenship Through Drama Education: The writings of Jonothan Neelands*. Stoke-on-Trent: Trentham Books.

— (1997) 'Beginning drama; 11–14'. In O'Connor, P. (ed.) (2010) *Creating Democratic Citizenship Through Drama Education: The writings of Jonothan Neelands*. Stoke-on-Trent: Trentham Books.

— (2000) 'In the hands of living people' *Drama Research*, 1 (March), 47–63. In O'Connor, P. (ed.) (2010) *Creating Democratic Citizenship Through Drama Education: The writings of Jonothan Neeland*. Stoke-on-Trent: Trentham Books.

— (2006) 'Mirror, dynamo or lens?'. In O'Connor, P. (ed.) (2010) *Creating Democratic Citizenship Through Drama Education: The writings of Jonothan Neelands*. Stoke-on-Trent: Trentham Books.

Neelands, J., and Goode, T. (2000) *Structuring Drama Work*. 2nd ed. Cambridge: Cambridge University Press.

Nicholson, H. (ed.) (2000) *Teaching Drama*. London: Continuum.

— (2005) *Applied Drama: The gift of theatre*. Basingstoke: Palgrave Macmillan.

— (2009) *Theatre and Education*. Basingstoke: Palgrave Macmillan.

— (2011) *Theatre, Education and Performance*. Basingstoke: Palgrave Macmillan.

O'Connor, P. (2010) *Creating Democratic Citizenship Through Drama Education: The writings of Jonothan Neelands*. Stoke-on-Trent: Trentham Books.

O'Neill, C. (1995) *Drama Worlds: A framework for process drama*. Portsmouth, NH: Heinemann.

O'Regan, T. (2004) *A Sense of Wonder: An introduction to drama in education*. Dublin: The Liffey Press.

O'Toole, J. (1992) *The Process of Drama: Negotiating art and meaning*. London: Routledge.

— (2002) 'Drama: The productive pedagogy'. *Melbourne Studies in Education*, 43 (2), 39–52. Cited in Anderson, M. (2012) *Master Class in Drama Education: Transforming teaching and learning*. London: Continuum.

O'Toole, J., and Haseman, B. (1998) *Dramawise: An introduction to GCSE drama*. London: Heinemann Educational Books.

O'Toole, J., and Stinson, M. (2009) 'Past, present and future: Which door next?' In O'Toole, J., Stinson, M., and Moore, T. *Drama and Curriculum: A giant at the door*. New York: Springer.

O'Toole, J., Stinson, M., and Moore, T. (2009) *Drama and Curriculum: A giant at the door*. New York: Springer.

Palast, G. (2002) *The Best Democracy Money Can Buy*. London: Robinson.

Pearson, R. (2005) *Voltaire Almighty: A life in pursuit of freedom*. London: Bloomsbury.

Piaget, J. (1972) *Play, Dreams and Imitation in Childhood*. London: Routledge and Kegan Paul.

Pilger, J. (2002) *The New Rulers of the World*. London: Verso.

Postman, N., and Weingartner, C. (1971) *Teaching as a Subversive Activity*. London: Penguin.

Prendergast, M., and Saxton, J. (eds) (2009) *Applied Theatre: International case studies and challenges for practice*. Bristol: Intellect.

Robinson, K. (2001) *Out of Our Minds: Learning to be creative*. Oxford: Capstone Press.

Sahlberg, P. (2011) *Finnish Lessons*. London: Teachers College Press.

Saul, J.R. (1993) *Voltaire's Bastards: The dictatorship of reason in the West*. New York: Vintage Books.

— (1997) *The Unconscious Civilization*. London: Penguin.

Schonmann, S. (ed.) (2011) *Key Concepts in Theatre/Drama Education*. Rotterdam: Sense Publishers.

Seymour, R. (2012) 'A short history of privatisation in the UK: 1979–2012'. *Guardian*, 29 March.

Stewart, H., and Treanor, J. (2012) 'Banking industry's year of shame ends in a blizzard of Libor revelations'. *Observer*, 23 December.

Tandy, M., and Howell, J. (2010) *Creating Drama with 7–11 Year Olds: Lesson ideas to integrate drama into the primary curriculum*. London: Routledge.

Taylor, P., and Warner, D. (eds) (2006) *Structure and Spontaneity: The process drama of Cecily O'Neill*. Stoke-on-Trent: Trentham Books.

Toye, N., and Prendiville, F. (2000) *Drama and Traditional Story for Early Years*. London: Routledge Falmer.

Toynbee, P., and Walker, D. (2012) *Dogma and Disarray: Cameron at half-time*. London: Granta.

Treanor, J. (2013) 'Banks Take Another Battering'. *Guardian*, 5 December.

Turner, V. (1982) *From Ritual to Theatre: The human seriousness of play*. New York: PAJ Publications.

Wagner, B.J. (1974) 'Evoking gut-level drama'. *Learning: The magazine for creative teaching* (US), March.

West, K. (2011) *Inspired Drama Teaching: A practical guide for teachers*. London: Continuum.

Wheeller, M. (2010) *Drama Schemes*. London: Rhinegold Education.

Willingham, D.T. (2009) *Why Don't Students Like School?: A cognitive scientist answers questions about how the mind works and what it means for the classroom*. San Francisco: Wiley.

Willingham, D. (2012) 'Did Michael Gove get the science right?' Online. www.danielwillingham.com/1/post/2012/11/did-michael-gove-get-the-science-right.html (accessed 13 February 2013).

Winston, J., and Tandy, M. (2001) *Beginning Drama 4–11*. 2nd ed. London: David Fulton Publishers.

Wolman, B. (1978) *Children's Fears*. New York: Grosset & Dunlap.

Woolland, B. (2008) *Pupils as Playwrights*. Stoke-on-Trent: Trentham Books.

— (2010) *Teaching Primary Drama*. Harlow: Longman.

Wooster, R. (2007) *Contemporary Theatre in Education*. Bristol: Intellect.

Žižek, S. (2008) *The Sublime Object of Ideology*. 2nd ed. London: Verso.

Index